KIHIVAS

Alone at the Ends of the Earth

ISTVAN KOPAR

with Robert Farrelly

Original cover design by Ernest Joe Gasis

Paperback cover design by Islam Farid

ISBN: 1517793637
ISBN-13: 978-1517793630

I dedicate this book to Zsuzsa and Piroska.
And to all those who were with me on my voyage,
and will be with me on those to come.

CONTENTS

If

If you can keep your head when all about you
Are losing theirs and blaming it on you,
If you can trust yourself when all men doubt you,
But make allowance for their doubting too;
If you can wait and not be tired by waiting,
Or being lied about, don't deal in lies,
Or being hated, don't give way to hating,
And yet don't look too good, nor talk too wise;
If you can dream—and not make dreams your master;
If you can think—and not make thoughts your aim;
If you can meet with Triumph and Disaster
And treat those two impostors just the same;
If you can bear to hear the truth you've spoken
Twisted by knaves to make a trap for fools,
Or watch the things you gave your life to, broken,
And stoop and build 'em up with worn-out tools;

If you can make one heap of all your winnings
And risk it on one turn of pitch-and-toss,
And lose, and start again at your beginnings
And never breathe a word about your loss;
If you can force your heart and nerve and sinew
To serve your turn long after they are gone,
And so hold on when there is nothing in you
Except the will which says to them: 'Hold on!'
If you can talk with crowds and keep your virtue,
Or walk with Kings—nor lose the common touch,
If neither foes nor loving friends can hurt you,
If all men count with you, but none too much;
If you can fill the unforgiving minute
With sixty seconds' worth of distance run,
Yours is the Earth and everything that's in it,
And—which is more—you'll be a Man, my son!

—Rudyard Kipling

"The majority of our fellow humans, upon reaching middle age, get used to the treadmill of life the way they know their ties every morning. How many of these people are among those who wanted to shape their lives according to their personalities, moreover they wanted to change the world a little. They don't know when and how they got rusted, when they became so worn as to fit into the packaging by the dozen. The ambition that fired them to reach their above average goals cooled unnoticed like a puppy love. This is the way they reached the state where the spirit of their youth—if resurrected—would feel in their grownup bodies like a ghost in an old castle refurbished by its owner with new furniture. There is no other property of the mind which has this secret transformation, commencing slowly, gradually. Their acquaintances, relatives contributed to this with the occasional contaminating breath, when during conversations they emphasized the lies of base accommodations, or presented the limited summaries of their sordid experiences, though sometimes the eyes of a woman blinded them so that they detoured from their selected path."

—Middlemarch, Northwest Passage, Chapter 2
(Kenneth Roberts)

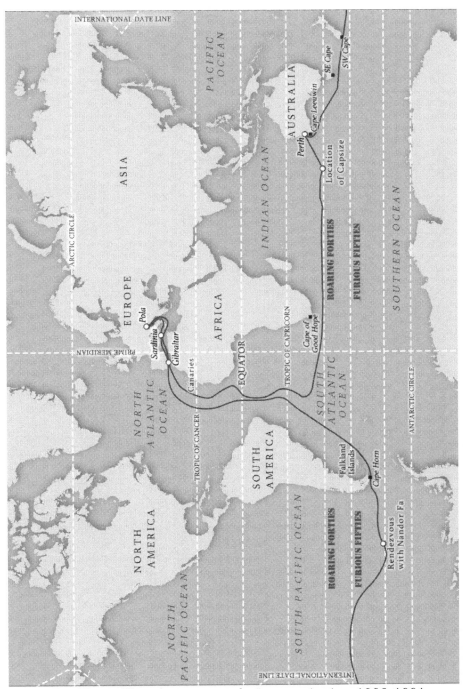

The route of Istvan Kopar's one-stop, solo circumnavigation, 1990-1991.

(Cartography by Jiban Dahal)

FOREWORD

Any dream can come true, if we are committed to it, and this book proves that. After thorough preparation over the course of 25 years, I took on the Seven Seas as the native of a landlocked country behind the Iron Curtain.

The outcome was literally life-changing; it reset my values and priorities, and ultimately altered even my homeland. However, I also lost my childhood dream in accomplishing it. I have been trying to fill up this resultant vacuum with new adventures for the past quarter-century. My second book, *Kihivas II: From the Szilas Creek to the Connecticut River*, is the chronicle of this period, covering many additional sea miles—including another circumnavigation—and a bumpy road on land.

Finally, there is hope on the horizon to reconnect with my lost childhood dream in the Golden Globe Race 2018, the ultimate solo circumnavigation. Of course I will not be able to surpass my previous performance at the age of 65, but it might once more grant me the limitless freedom that can only be found at the Roaring Forties and Furious Fifties, in the home of the albatrosses. I hope this book will serve as your guide to this unique region, the last frontier of freedom.

Let me finish my introduction with a quote from one of my favorite writers, Mark Twain: *"Twenty years from now you will be more disappointed by the things that you didn't do than by the ones you did do. So throw off the bowlines. Sail away from the safe harbor. Catch the Trade Winds in your sails. Explore. Dream. Discover."*

—*Istvan Kopar*

September 2015

1

THE OCEAN CALLS AND WAITS

"There is no destination. The voyage itself is the destination."
—Paul Geraldy

JUNE 1990

THE SWITCHBACKS LEADING TO THE ISTRIAN PENINSULA swept lower and lower as our small car slowly crossed the Karst Mountains of Yugoslavia. The driver had to be especially careful watching out for the sharp turns while keeping an eye on the laboring truck in front of us, transporting *Salammbo* on its trailer. It was getting more difficult to concentrate on the road and the vehicle at the same time.

Many times the waves of excitement swept over me. At last, I gazed upon the view I had been anticipating. As the mountains finally gave way, the sea appeared before us. The Adriatic lazed in its best colors in the Bay of Fiume on that early afternoon in June. Its slowly rolling blue meadows dissolved into fog in the distance. I had seen it before as rough, gray, and stormy, but it had always fascinated me. It reminded me that my contact with the sea was much more than a simple aesthetic experience. It had been the place of my existence for a decade and a half. I can still remember when it all began...

* * *

It was summer then as well... the summer of 1970. The young man with the cropped brown hair excitedly pressed his forehead to the cool window of the compartment as the train sped through the Karst Mountains. From

15

time to time he opened the window, to relieve the fever caused by the numerous inoculations he had just received. It was the first excursion out of the country for the vacationing high school student. Yet somehow he had a feeling that many more such adventures awaited him in the future, deepening his connection with the sea.

As the train descended to the Bay of Fiume, the boy's thrill over the proximity of the vast waters pushed the throbbing pain of his punctured arm into the background. His curiosity wasn't triggered by the water alone, but more by the ships. The port wasn't yet visible, but the bay was occupied by oceangoing ships, anchored and waiting to be loaded. The sight of these vessels completed his joy at encountering the sea for the first time in his life.

It was another three months before our young hero opened the window of the train again—now with calloused hands—to wave goodbye to his new friends the seamen.[1] He had grown to a man over the summer vacation he spent as a deck boy on the M/V *Borsod*[2]. He predicted correctly that his new bond with the sea would have a decisive impact on his whole life. His future would be linked with that of the Hungarian Merchant Marine. The MAHART shipping company[3] was a method of escaping Hungary's borders to see the world, which was a unique opportunity at that time in an Eastern European country. The application process was so highly selective that it was more difficult to secure a berth with MAHART than to be admitted to the best university in the country. Even for the lowest position, there were fewer than five hundred openings. The minimum requirements included a high school diploma, aptitude and psychological tests, and a thorough physical examination.

Naturally, those who were fortunate enough to be accepted wanted to preserve their privileged status, and the price of doing so in those times was honest hard work. The traditions of the pre-World War II years still had their influence, and experts in the old companies taught and educated the new generation. Those working on ships of the Merchant Marine, who were

---

[1] In this book I use the term "seaman" to refer to merchant mariners working on ships, while I use the term "sailor" to describe the skippers or crew of sailboats.

[2] The prefix "M/V" is short for "Motor Vessel" and is used to distinguish so-called steamers (aka diesel-powered vessels), as opposed to wind-powered vessels.

[3] MAHART (MHRT), an acronym for the Hungarian Shipping Company (Magyar Hajózási Részvénytársaság), was the only shipping company allowed in Hungary at the time. Since it engaged in trade with various capitalist countries, it intentionally had the "RT" part of the name (indicating it had shareholders) to give the impression that it was a private company, even though it was in fact state-owned. MAHART had five branches, including among them a seagoing branch, lake shipping branch, and river shipping branch.

always away on extended voyages, were lucky that they did not have to suffer through what the general population of Eastern Europe was forced to endure. The trade of the mariner could be pursued under more suitable circumstances, because merchant seamanship is a demanding and sometimes dangerous occupation. In most career fields, people were chosen for jobs based on their degree of loyalty to the Communist Party. Fortunately this system was not possible in the merchant marine, in which seamen had to be truly experienced and qualified to have any chance of surviving in the trade. It was the era when sea captains spoke five languages and knew all maritime laws. Party-inspired personnel selection (based on political "reliability") would only later show its destructive effects in our line of work. But on board M/V *Borsod* the respected values were still honest work and camaraderie, as well as love of country, profession, and family. This conservative order of values, combined with the strict hierarchy of the chain of command, ensured the discipline that is always demanded by the extreme requirements of seagoing.

In my seventeenth year, I could not yet comprehend the political situation within the Hungarian Merchant Marine, but I could discern true values from sham (this talent of mine would later get me into some conflicts). My instinct for knowing what was right stemmed from my previous sailing experience, for I had not been a greenhorn landlubber when I first embarked in Fiume. I had lived near water and boats since I was just a few months old. Everybody in my family sailed, and they do so to this day. My attraction for the water led to many close calls over the years, but the Lord somehow always saved me. First it was in the person of Uncle Kamatler. It was he who dragged me out of the deep bay of the clubhouse in Almadi, where as a five-year-old I made my debut in near-drowning. I had similar experiences on the icy Lake Balaton, at the waterfall of Lillafüred, and in the Szilas Creek, where I jumped from a railroad bridge. It was clearly evident early on that I was not going to be a sedentary type.

In addition to my adventurous ramblings, I always found time for reading exciting books. It should come as no surprise that after devouring the works of James Fenimore Cooper, Karl May, and Jules Verne, I moved on to those of András Dekany, the famous Hungarian writer of sailing novels. By the light of my reading lamp, I voyaged on the high seas under the command of Hornblower, Wandellar, and Nelson.

I was twelve years old when I got my first sailboat, the *Red Fox*. The boat was nearly thirty years old, a well experienced "Pirate" type,[4] and really only half mine—but I don't remember any other present in my whole

---

[4] "Pirate" type sailboats were small, old-fashioned wooden dinghies of German design. They had a huge open cockpit and were mostly used on lakes.

Above: *My first bow job, working under Mom's supervision.*

Above: *Further training with Dad, in his Star, Lake Balaton, 1958.*

Above: *Racing already, in a club Star at this time, 1971.*

Above: *My very first Lifeboat Exercise on board the M/V Borsod, 1970.*

Above: *And so it continued, on to larger ships and higher ranks…*
(Here as a deckhand on board the M/S Raba, 1972.)

Above: *As a cadet on board the M/V Debrecen, 1979—I sailed on cargo vessels during the summer break of my maritime university years. I am shown here with a shark I caught while we were anchored in the Red Sea, waiting for our turn to dock in harbor.*

life that gave me such happiness. My fellow club members in Balatonalmádi know how much I loved my subsequent boats, but my first notable accomplishments were achieved at the tiller of the *Red Fox*. Among these were the Almadi-Csopak-Almadi sail (approximately 12 miles), and my week-long circumnavigation of Lake Balaton (approximately 115 miles). The *Red Fox* was followed by younger and sportier boats. But they belonged to the next chapter of my life, when racing was center stage.

So when I first stepped onto the hot and rusty deck of the vessel *Borsod* as a seventeen-year-old, I could distinguish the stern from the stem, and I had an idea of the skills involved in running a ship. My favorite novels did not misrepresent the truth; their heroes resembled the seamen I met, so I was happy to put on the uniform of a merchant mariner. The only downside was that I had to walk away from active racing at the worst time for a competitor—I had been winning.

I was compensated with eventful sailing years. In my first thirteen years with MAHART, I visited fifty countries, and advanced through the proper certifications. My training on the International Radio-Telecommunication course was followed by studying at the Budapest Technical University, where I majored in Maritime Studies.[5] It was during that period that the effects of political degradation reached the bastions of seagoing shipping. The company's privileged status quickly disappeared as modern ships with "push-button efficiency" meant that skills and experience at sea no longer had as much value. The personnel were soon diluted with incompetent political appointees. Absurd ideological discussions were introduced. In a trade in which some assignments were more desirable than others, appointments to destinations started being decided purely on the basis of political loyalty. Cliques sprang up in different branches. The quality of work and the condition of the ships rapidly declined. Before the total collapse could occur, I had to disembark from the ship *Petőfi* due to a family tragedy. In consideration of my family's wishes, as well as the deterioration of the conditions in the seafaring industry, I chose not to rejoin. I pursued my livelihood on land for a while, until I came upon my ultimate plan—judged to be madness by many— along with the instrument needed to achieve it: *Salammbo*.

* * *

---

[5] Budapest Technical University was a very prestigious institution. Maritime operator certification was required in order to operate nautical shipping. International radio-telecommunication required learning Morse Code, which was only transmitted in English (meanwhile, the legal code I had to learn was in French). The radio telephone was barely used at that time due to the likelihood of miscommunication.

OUR TROUBLES ON DRY LAND

The boat rocked and rolled on the bed of the 16-wheeler in front of us. On some turns I could see its entire orange-red hull, while my mind, like an x-ray machine, saw the inside of the 31-foot Balaton model. I could picture the main cabin, a few square meters in area, the chart table, the small galley with the gimbaled gas range, the bunks, and the rows of instruments. I knew exactly what was crammed into the boat, from the provisions to the life raft. Even then, so close to the start, it seemed strange that I should trust my life to that little "nutshell," as we would say in Hungarian. For an entire year around the world, with only one landfall in 35,000 miles, this sailboat would be more than a home. It would be my place of work, my refuge from the elements, and might even become—heaven forbid—my own coffin.

There were four of us in the car following the transport truck. In the back seat was Peter Szabó, an active Merchant Marine Captain who had been my companion on the *Petöfi* on the waters of the Far East. On his vacation time, against his family's wishes, he had volunteered to sail with me to Cagliari in Sardinia. Any problems with the boat would hopefully become evident during this shakedown cruise, and then I should be able to cope with the Mediterranean shipping traffic on my own from Cagliari to Gibraltar.

Behind me sat Dezso Balogh, one of *Salammbo*'s "fathers." He was someone with the nature to always accept the news of disasters without batting an eye. And we had all experienced our share of disasters. Living proof was Jancsi Radics, squeezed into the seat beside me. His face and ears were full of cuts and bruises, and his movements were still unnaturally stiff. His beautiful Ford minivan, which was supposed to have transported us to Pola, had been completely wrecked two weeks earlier. On his way home after visiting me, he had stopped for a hitchhiker and was rear-ended by a bus. Jancsi had gone to the hospital, and the Ford to the scrapyard.

"Never mind," Lajos Ruhl, one of my sailor friends, had said. He would transport us to the harbor in Pola instead of Jancsi. Unfortunately, when he was running around trying to arrange some of my affairs, an improper movement had pinched one of his nerves, nearly paralyzing him. In the meantime, Jancsi Radics had left the hospital and defiantly declared that even if we went with my car, he would be the driver. My sponsor, the Ganz-Danubius Trading Company, updated the travel arrangements—now for the third time—without any complaint.

My friends assured me that a trip that started with so many misfortunes must end well. I would very much need their optimism, because fate still held a few surprises. I had arranged for my friend with the transport truck, Bela Herczeg, to meet us in the Ganz-Danubius shipyard in Balatonfüred three days before my departure. Instead, a messenger arrived telling us that Bela's truck had crashed the day before and he was having problems as a result. What could we do? It was Friday afternoon. The shift would be finished shortly and the crane could not be used again before Monday, but I was expected in Pola. Before we had time to go crazy, a miracle happened. The gate opened and Bela Herczeg, in elegant white overalls, drove a shiny new trailer rig under the crane. Our breath stopped... Imposing dimensions, a dozen steerable wheels... If I had known about this ahead of time, I would have built a bigger boat!

The spectacle of the truck's appearance surprised even the sun, which withdrew behind a raincloud as the crane lifted *Salammbo* skyward. We got thoroughly drenched in the ensuing downpour, and could not even take photographs. After quickly tying up all the fastenings, we said goodbye to the shipyard people.

Above: *The beginning of the departure, difficult even from the boatyard.*

But it had been a premature farewell. Turning onto Highway 71, the truck bottomed out, and then a real show started. The blocked stream of cars trying to hurry to Lake Balaton for the weekend created a colossal traffic jam. The shipyard's towing rig plus the helpful driver of a German tourist bus failed to budge our stranded truck. At least the bus passengers had the chance to take photos and video as they finally witnessed some action. The end of the traffic jam ran all the way to the village of Csopak two miles away, with volunteer traffic controllers trying to maintain order. We needed another miracle, and it finally arrived in the form of a heavy

Tatra towing vehicle.

The boat eventually started its overland trip, until we had to stop at the town limits of Balatonfüred. The truck's many pairs of steerable wheels decided to go their own separate way, which was unfortunately not the way of the road. We could not give up! A few hundred pumps on the hydraulic jacks and another half hour later, we reached Almadi. There was hardly time to catch our breath, with only one day to pack everything into the boat.

What *Salammbo* took for its yearlong trip was no small potatoes. Into its holds and tanks went 1300 pounds of food, 80 gallons (96 U.S.)[6] of water, 55 gallons (66 U.S.) of diesel, and two 10-pint gas cylinders. We loaded the clothing and books, and found a place for the tools and all of the other equipment. The inventory was continuously updated as additional items appeared all the time. In the evening, Valter Speer, the manager of the Ganz-Danubius Trading Company, arrived with a satellite navigator fresh from the Customs people. My friend Zoltan Konkoly—the builder of the boat's electronics and electrical systems—looked at the thick manual, and we exchanged glances. He rushed home for his tools and a quick meal, as I went to find an English technical dictionary. I had reckoned that I wouldn't sleep in a regular bed for another year, but I never thought that it would start right here in Almadi. Installation continued through the night.

At dawn everybody was still hard at work. The boat stood on its trailer between the service road and Route 71, beside the Videoton clubhouse. The army of relatives, friends, and well-wishers was a help, but their work needed direction and coordination. Their crowding around with numerous inquiries developed into a show. The local market merchants were probably sorry that they had not received prior notification. By the afternoon I had become somewhat frustrated. Later I had to apologize to those I had unintentionally offended. The next day Jancsi Radics solved the problem; he simply did not let anybody come near me. His visible head wounds from the recent car accident proved to be a very effective deterrent in his role as my bodyguard.

It was difficult to believe, but by Sunday evening everything was in the boat and ready to go. The traveling group gathered in the nearby Ottila Restaurant for a group dinner, which my less optimistic friends labeled my Last Supper. The relaxed atmosphere lasted only until we discovered that some necessary documents had been left behind in Budapest. I wasn't even surprised at that point. Two of my friends drove to Budapest while the boat started toward the border.

After spending seven hours at the border—an experience not worth

---

[6] Note that my use of "gallons" refers to British gallons, each equal to approximately 1.2 U.S. gallons.

detailing—we finally made it to the Istrian Peninsula. Heading our convoy was a Yugoslav official guide who was friendly and helpful, but unfortunately not familiar with the highways of Istria. One wrong turn was enough to get us completely lost. Bad roads were followed by worse ones, with one switchback after another. Someone always had to run ahead to measure the clearance at underpasses. And although the night was cool, we all kept dozing off behind the wheel.

At one point Jancsi Radics became annoyed by the yellow flashing light at the end of the trailer in front of us. During a slowdown to climb a hill he stepped out of the car, ran ahead, and hung his cap on the light. We found it an ingenious solution, until a car behind us started honking to call our attention to the flaming cap. Thank God we were able to stop the truck and the fire in time—our spare cans of gasoline were in the area just below the yellow light.

After a journey that seemed to last forever, our convoy entered the seaside city of Pola, Yugoslavia.[7] We stopped a stone's throw away from the Roman amphitheater, in the parking lot of the Uljanik shipyard. I had to tighten my coat in the cold air. Just before falling into a deep sleep, I thought apprehensively, "What will happen to you on the sea, *Salammbo*, if things continue the way they started on the land?"

UNFURLING THE SAILS ON THE ADRIATIC

Pola, the southernmost city of the Istrian Peninsula—with its picturesque harbor, row of hotels, romantic bays, and its historic marvel, the Roman amphitheater—has always been one of the most popular tourist attractions of the Istrian coast. The older generations remember it for different reasons. For them, Pola was the main base of the Austro-Hungarian Navy's fleet. My choice for the starting point of the journey could have been made in honor of those traditions alone, but I had also made the decision on the basis of practicality. In Pola I could count on the help of friends, especially the Hungarians who worked there. My enthusiastic sponsor, the Ganz-Danubius Company, introduced me to the firm of Matrapack, which had 150 Hungarians working in their Uljanik shipyard.

The reception for *Salammbo* exceeded all my expectations. The dynamic arranger of the details had been Istvan Tozser, the local representative of Ganz-Danubius. He proved to be an experienced trade representative and a good friend. I was indebted to him for introducing me to Walter Klobasz, the shipyard's extremely helpful managing director.

---

[7] The official spelling of "Pola" or "Pula" has changed throughout history. Although both spellings are now accepted, "Pula" is generally used more often today. I have deliberately chosen to use the old-fashioned "Pola" spelling throughout this book as a nod to its important role in Austro-Hungarian history. Though part of Croatia since 1991, the city was part of Yugoslavia at the time.

Anything I asked of Istvan was promptly fulfilled. In the offices of the Port Authorities, we successfully fought bureaucratic dragons and completed the paperwork required by Customs and Health authorities. Only then were we able to look for a safe harbor.

The police escorted us to the splendid yacht harbor of the Uljanik shipyard, where the factotum of the yard's yacht club, Charlie, awaited us. The thickset, deeply tanned man, emanating an aroma of Slivovic, immediately won our trust. As soon as he spotted us, he demonstrated his readiness to help by rushing to remove the small barricade from the entrance. Our communication was aided by a special Mediterranean cocktail—not a drink in this case, but a mix of Italian and English harbor language, which made our conversations quite delightful. We did not have to explain anything to all-heart Charlie; he could always read our thoughts.

We coated the bottom of the boat with anti-fouling paint and sought out charts, flags, and a crane. After one day of hard work, *Salammbo* was bobbing on the bay's waters. The launching came at a good time. Timing their Yugoslav holiday well, my in-laws had just arrived in Pola, along with my 13-year-old daughter Piroska. They parked their motor home in the campground of the nearby Stoja peninsula, and so the trailer camp's harbor became the first destination on *Salammbo*'s shakedown cruise.

The countless activities of the previous days had made us forget the significance of the event: it was *Salammbo*'s first sail. I remember setting the course towards Stoja in sunshine and good winds. Yet I was somewhat disheartened, because the boat moved as slowly as a retired old lady as it sailed out of the bay. Even boats of inferior design flew past us like darting seagulls. I cheered up with the realization that we were six people crammed into a ship laden with half a year's worth of supplies. Not to mention that one of those passengers was Bela Herczeg, who, like his truck, is double-sized.

We dropped anchor near the campsite in Stoja, and with war cries we leapt into the blue bay. We raced for the shore with great strokes. Every participant in this impromptu swimming contest received his proper prize: my relatives on shore greeted us with an excellent selection of drinks. My daughter sat on my lap with her arms around my neck as I looked out at the water. For the first time in years, after all the hustling and apprehension, I was able to relax as I rested my eyes on *Salammbo* floating on the water in the golden sunshine.

The following day, Friday the 15th of June, we started the countdown. In the midst of all the activities it slowly dawned on me that I would be gone for a year and left all to myself. I had planned my departure for Saturday, but the goodbyes had already begun. The well-wishers arrived one after another: friends, acquaintances, and even complete strangers, who had been cued by a radio announcement about *Salammbo*'s departure. The minutes and hours of the farewell would be etched into my memory forever, to be recalled in times of need and despair.

After we sailed *Salammbo* to Pola's duty-free pier, a few Italian and Yugoslav reporters pounced on me. At the same time my friend and business partner, Stefan Aschenbrenner, arrived with a four-member delegation from Ganz-Danubius. The former and the latter had each brought me a life raft. Stefan's gift was a six-person raft laden with provisions, but heavy. When I pointed out my overloaded boat's disappearing water line, my friend understood that even though I deeply appreciated the concern he demonstrated, I had to choose the lighter raft. A new friend and gift arrived, as Dr. Geza Guszter surprised me with a radar detector. This handy and expensive instrument sounds an alarm when receiving another ship's radar emissions. On busy waterways it is an invaluable piece of equipment. Geza and his wife had come all the way from Denmark to bid farewell to me in Pola.

Denes Miltenyi, the manager of Matrapack, had just jammed the entrance with his basket of gifts when along came Jozsef Gal, who was one of *St. Jupat*'s crew members[8] and also the president of the Equator Club. Jozsi had previously offered to help with *Salammbo*. The two highly skilled radio hams[9] of the Equator Club, Zsolt Pál and Karoly Nyemcsek, were to follow me on the airwaves for a year. The experience that the *St. Jupat* had gained during its circumnavigation guaranteed that the radio connection to the land would be well organized. Jozsi Gal arrived with Karoly Nyemcsek, who gave a brief greeting before immediately taking over *Salammbo*'s radio set and burying himself deeply in radio work. Radio hams are probably the only enthusiasts more possessed than single-handers; that's why we understood each other so well.

Fortunately the constant stream of visitors prevented me from becoming too sentimental. It had gotten late, and I needed to hurry to the farewell dinner. I actually had to switch the equipment off to drag Karcsi away from the radio. He resisted to the last minute as he exchanged some last pieces of information with another radio ham from the Kerguelen Islands.

On Saturday, June 16, I got up at dawn. The rays of the rising sun ricocheted like a billiard ball between the surface of the bay's water and the windows of the buildings on the shore. The play of light was broken only by the dark windowless mass of the amphitheater. There was no breeze at all… real churchgoing weather. I was about to embark on a less peaceful voyage with *Salammbo*, but I hoped that the Lord would be with me there as

---

[8] The *St. Jupat* was a 31-foot yacht that circumnavigated the globe with a Hungarian crew, 1986-87.

[9] "radio hams": aka amateur radio operators

well.

Together in silence, Peter Szabó and I decorated the boat with flags. On the mast, we raised a worn but precious flag that would serve as club pennant. It was a flag with important historical significance. I had obtained it from the well-guarded safe of the Nemzeti Hajos Egylet (Hungarian National Boating Association) founded by Istvan Szechenyi in 1841. The newly revived club had asked me, on the occasion of the 150th anniversary of its founding, to take the pennant on my circumnavigation. I was deeply moved by their trust in me.

People started to arrive as the festivities began. A dozen small Optimist sailboats bobbed along in the water, circling *Salammbo* like bridesmaids around a bride. The shipyard personnel, both Hungarians and Puloians, arrived one after another. Amid the circle of my friends I saw Walter Klobas, the chief engineer of Uljanik, and the all-heart Charlie. A representative from the firm Hempel shoved a bottle of good whiskey under my arm. Denes Miltenyi generously gave me some spending money and shook my hand in encouragement. Jozsef Gal, who had previously shared so much with me about his own circumnavigating experiences, now simply said, "Fair winds!"[10] Janos Kovacs, alias Szines, had arrived with his wife in the early morning straight from Monte Carlo. He was the president of *Salammbo* Sport Club and my longtime friend. I knew that he would have liked to come along with me, and that he had difficulty swallowing the idea of my solo undertaking. As the next best thing to actually accompanying me, he had immersed himself in helping with the preparations.

The crews of the Zagrab and Hungarian Sun TV stations got ready, as radio reporters and Italian journalists also started to arrive. They moved me around like a marionette according to their scripts, making me feel eager to start my trip early. Yet I was grateful for their orchestrations; they made it easier to hide the tears that were occasionally shining in my eyes.

My friends released my dock lines at exactly 10:00am, and the boat slowly moved away with the light wind. The young captains of the Optimists guided their dinghies like graceful cygnets alongside *Salammbo*. I fired a flare, and my horn was answered by those of the other ships in the harbor. Peter and I had to watch the buoys, which fortunately helped to turn my head in the right direction. As we reached the island of the shipyard, 150 voices resonated, "HUNGARIA!" That was too much for me to take. I gave the helm to Peter, and found things for myself to do in the cabin. I reached reflexively into my pocket, where I found the creation of my sister-in-law and nephew. It was a poem with a (for me, unfortunately

---

[10] Exact translation of the Hungarian would be "Good Winds!", though in English the meaning would be closer to "Fair Winds!", or "Smooth Sailing!"

meaningless) musical score: *(Note: Adapted by my daughters from the original Hungarian.)*

Easy it is to begin a journey,
Returning home is the victory.
Battling the titanic winds
Is a testing trajectory.

Dreams can and do come true
You sail across the Seven Seas
Your small boat as your heroine
The world is now yours to seize.

Solitary in your vessel
Loneliness you cannot feel
Your family and many friends
Cheer you on with hearts of zeal.

God is always on your side
This will be your fortitude
Our prayers are without bounds
These we'll send in multitude.

All who have tried to overcome
To go beyond their own limits
All who at this have tried their hand
With respect and awe they stand.

Our trust is in you Captain
But for your safety we do fear
You will return, for you well know
A little girl longs for when you're near.

I returned to take the helm. Though it required great effort, I did not look back at the well-wishers in the distance.

2

ON THE SEAS OF MY NIGHTMARES

"Life was created in the valleys. It blew up onto the hills on the old terrors, the old lusts, the old despairs. That's why you must walk up the hills so you can ride down."

—William Faulkner, *As I Lay Dying*

IT WAS TWO THOUSAND MILES FROM ISTRIA TO GIBRALTAR, the official start of my circumnavigation. Peter and I embarked upon our prearranged plan, by which *Salammbo* would sail down the Adriatic, circle the Italian boot, traverse the Straits of Messina, and then head west across the Mediterranean to the gate of the Atlantic. On the Adriatic the currents run counterclockwise, so we followed the Italian shore going south. It was a bare and unimpressive section of coastline that we could have passed in a hurry with good winds propelling us and the waves in the right direction. Instead, calm conditions caused us to cool our heels in the first few days. To further try our patience, the wind vane—which was supposed to hold the boat on course—could not function properly in the variable breezes, so one of us had to steer at all times.[11] In the daytime we were both up, and we

---

[11] To the average landlubber, a "wind vane" is an instrument used to indicate the wind direction. In this context, however, it refers to a device that can actually be rigged to keep a sailboat on a set course. When working properly, the wind vane will adjust the rudder as needed to keep the boat on the same heading, even if the wind direction changes. Having a wind vane enables the skipper to cook or sleep in the cabin while the boat continues sailing in the proper direction. It is an essential tool for the singlehanded sailor to have, though it must be emphasized that this device is not without its limitations.

took turns on four-hour watches throughout the night.

Even though the professed objective of my enterprise was to circumnavigate the globe singlehanded within one year, with only one stop, during this first stretch of the journey from Pola I was in the company of an active sea captain. Originally I had planned to make Pola the official start and endpoint of my solo voyage, but the route was abbreviated by the usual restrictions—lack of money and time. Nonetheless, the overall degree of difficulty was still intact.

Our globe can be circumnavigated with a small sailboat by many different methods, but as far as I know, nobody has done it without a shakedown cruise first. Regardless, that was the case for me. To avoid appearing reckless, I had decided it was best to make the trip to Gibraltar with a shipmate. (Unfortunately, wanting for both time and a visa, Peter could only be with me until Cagliari in Sardinia.) My decision had been dictated by the lack of autopilot, without which solo navigating is rarely undertaken these days. Additionally, the likelihood of a great volume of shipping traffic in all directions on the Mediterranean argued that I should make the start and endpoint of the voyage at Gibraltar. Hence while the journey for *Salammbo* and her captain started in Pola, the Pola-Gibraltar section was merely part of the preparatory phase.

The sail from Pola to Cagliari had a few unpleasant surprises for us, despite the fact that both of us had already sailed a great deal in this area on big ships. Nothing extraordinary happened; it was simply that we were forced to adopt a new way of life. After the first few days, we learned that this kind of sailing was far different from our experiences with the merchant marine at sea, or sailing on Lake Balaton at home. A sailor is worried mostly about storms and calms. Here on the sea, both were on a whole new scale. On the Adriatic and the Mediterranean, we mostly experienced the latter.

We had to accustom ourselves to the unpleasant motion of the boat, and the tight living space in the small cabin crammed with equipment. As a sailor, I actually have to confess that I was bothered by the saltwater more than anything else. Just think of how the salt in a salt shaker sticks together in damp weather—the same thing happened to all of our sea-soaked clothing. In vain we dried it during the day, for in the evening mist it always became sticky again. We had years of experience going to sea on commercial ships, and now we were forcibly reminded that even the smallest seagoing ship with minimal facilities can still provide the comfort of land living. But sailing on a small yacht, right on the level of the water, was a completely different experience. We needed to invent a new way of living on our boat, and adapt ourselves to the rhythm and spirit of the sea.

THE ART OF SAFETY

The frustratingly weak winds of the Adriatic did not let me forget that I was preparing myself for the stormy seas of the Southern Oceans, where I would probably wish to be back in this blue and placidly undulating sea. Naturally, the Adriatic and Mediterranean might just as easily surprise us. For that reason, as well as the live-in routine, my first task was to inspect the safety equipment. I had obtained most of it at the last minute, and I had to learn how to use it all.

Books about sailing usually have a chapter concerning man overboard and how to prevent it from happening. The proven tool is the harness, which is fastened around the upper torso and tethered to a strong point on the deck. Because this "umbilical cord" usually restricts normal motion, I fixed a line behind the railing on both sides of the deck from the bow's pulpit to the stern. Clipping onto one of these safety lines, I was able to move from front to back with relative safety. I forced myself right from the beginning to get accustomed to using the harness at all times, so that in an emergency it would be an automatic reflex to do so.

The most important piece of safety equipment, the life raft I had received in Pola, was fixed on deck behind the mast. Normally encased in a plastic container, the raft automatically inflates in the event of a sinking, or if thrown into the water. The covered raft had storage for flares, signal lights, a Morse mirror, a sea anchor, fishing equipment, and 5 liters of water. I thought this supply to be inadequate, so I had also packed a water resistant sack with an extra 10-liter water bottle, a diver's knife with a light, fishing lines, warm waterproof garments, and a flotation jacket. A hand-operated watermaker went into the bag too. This expensive apparatus can use the process of osmosis to extract one glass of drinking water out of seawater after ten minutes of pumping. The pockets of my waterproof suits were filled with NATO bars. The NATO bar is a high-calorie nonperishable soy product packaged in waterproof wrapping, made for the military by the Budapesti Edesipari Vallalat. I kept the well-packed bag in a safe place, to be readily available in case of an emergency.

Back in Pola we had shackled the two radar reflectors to the top shrouds, close to the masthead. I had to rearrange the angles of the aluminum plates of the reflectors because the jib halyard often caught against them. A fiberglass sailboat gives a weak reflection on the radar screens of other boats, so their correct placement was very important. I placed one of my fire extinguishers below the companionway, and the other beside the chart table. I also stowed a steel axe and a bayonet there. I still had to find a place for the flares, flare gun, and gas-operated horn, and to affix the waterproof battery-operated and kerosene storm lights in different locations. Without the help of my primary sponsor, the Magyar Hitel Bank (Hungarian Credit Bank), my safety equipment inventory would have been far too short. Now I had to spend several hours each day locating, checking, and arranging all of it. Even more time was needed to inspect my navigation instruments. The major part of my boat's library consisted of technical manuals and user guides.

The satellite navigator was a novelty for me. Its use makes determination of the ship's position very easy. Using signals from satellites, the instrument can pinpoint the position of the boat to an accuracy of a couple hundred meters. For that reason we used it even in coastal piloting. Piloting was further helped by two other instruments, a digital compass equipped with memory and stopwatch, and 7x50 binoculars with built-in compass.

Besides the modern equipment, I was equipped with traditional navigational instruments that I would be able to use in all circumstances. My thin wallet dictated the choice of the classical instrument, the sextant. I bought the Davis Master, the cheapest plastic model, along with a navigational computer containing astronomical data. It soon became evident, following some trial measurements, that the mirrors of the sextant moved too much and the measurements were inaccurate. For a chronometer, I used a waterproof Citizen Quartz watch. Navigation was also assisted by an ultrasonic depth sounder. In spite of my financial restraints, I felt that *Salammbo* was equipped with everything needed for a safe circumnavigation. I could not have predicted then that the lovingly stored instruments would all fail one after the other. I could just as well have dumped them at the beginning of the voyage.

OUR PLEASURES ON LAND

We had enough to do on the deck, but more and more time was needed for handling the boat. After we left Vieste, the first Italian city on the coast that could be called pretty, the wind turned against us. The Levanter blowing from ahead did not quite reach the "storm" grade on the Beaufort Scale, but the suddenly choppy sea caused *Salammbo* to pitch and heave. The sails had to be reefed on the heeling boat, and doing it for the first time required much time and effort.[12] Unfortunately, the sails had arrived at the last minute, making practicing impossible. It was a novelty to me to have reefing points on the headsail to allow reduction of its size, similar to on the mainsail.

At the end, wet and tired, but satisfied with the results of the task, I climbed back to the helm. Peter offered me a glass of "Zwack Unicum" as a

---

[12] Reefing is a technique in sailing that is necessary sometimes in very strong winds, and especially in stormy conditions, in order to keep the boat under control. The area of a sail that is exposed to the wind is decreased by rolling or folding the sail at its base. Reefing techniques vary depending on the design of the sail, but some sails have "reef points" specifically fashioned for this purpose.

bonus for the job well done.[13] We emptied the glasses to our health. The drinks buoyed us up. Under the reduced sail plan, *Salammbo* danced on the increasing waves. With the passing of time, and the effect of the drinks, our enthusiasm abated. We had been sailing within the sight of shore, our eyes searching for harbors. After only five days, we were already craving a hot shower, a flat bed, and a dinner served on a motionless table.

The magnetic variation in our sailing area was negligible, but we deviated from the planned course and approached the shore. Our practice had always been to adapt to every situation. Reinforced by more Unicum, we decided that it would be most uncivil to miss paying a visit to the daughter of one of my acquaintances who lived in Bari. Fortunately we found a sailboat heading towards Bari, and since we lacked the detailed charts, we followed it. We had bet on the right horse, because instead of the overpriced yacht harbor, we were guided into the premises of a friendly yacht club.

There was only one empty slip, and the owner of a fishing boat encouraged us to tie up. Our overloaded boat grounded, and it took a lot of maneuvering with the docking lines to tie it up. From the neighboring yacht we phoned Aniko, my friend's daughter, but because of the late hour we could only report our presence.

The real pleasures came after that. Reborn from a shower under a hose from a garden spigot, we headed for the nearest open air restaurant, stumbling along on the too-smooth level pavement. We satisfied our hunger with an excellent supper, knowing that we and our boat had reached safety.

The following day, well rested on the idle boat, we set about the activities on our job list with great vigor. Peter washed the boat while I tuned the rigging. The wind and waves on the Adriatic showed that the sea required a much tighter rigging than Lake Balaton. I fine-tuned the running rigging and rigged preventers on the mainsail, modified the reefing lines, and tried to make the portholes watertight. We put lee cloths on the bunks to prevent me from falling out of bed. Whenever we needed it, the owners of the neighboring boats happily offered their help.

That evening, all dressed up and carrying Gyulai sausage and the Unicum as agreed, we started towards a small, genuine South Italian restaurant. The father of my friend Antonio, as befitting the head of a clan, treated us in true style with the local specialties. Thanks to my seafaring years, the courses based on the fruits-de-mar were to be expected, but we had never anticipated such an abundant and well served meal. The waiters gained my appreciation for changing the dishes of fish, clams, scallops, and

---

[13] "Zwack Unicum": a popular Hungarian liqueur

shrimp so swiftly that I was unable to eat enough to make me sick!

The next day, Antonio took us shopping, causing more unease with his sporty driving than the storm on the Adriatic ever could. A bigger unease waited for us in the marine store when I saw the prices. My purse was flattened after buying only a few minor items. But I had enriched *Salammbo*'s supplies with a nonstick frying pan, a dish-drying rack, plastic containers, long-life bread, and a gallon of cheap wine from a neighboring supermarket.

In the evening we were visited by the captain of a nearby schooner, *Four Clouds*. His experienced eyes immediately saw that *Salammbo* was at the start of an extraordinary voyage. He wanted to give me a spare compass, but I could not accept it. So instead he gave me, as a charm, a stainless steel shackle from the supplies of his 76-year-old boat. That evening we visited our new friend on board his wonderful two-master. To the joy of his numerous children, we had brought a large piece of milk chocolate in thanks for the shackle.

According to my log, we left the harbor of Bari on Saturday, June 23, at 10:30am. We sailed the rest of the Adriatic in variable northerlies, most of them weak. We enjoyed spotlessly clean skies, deep blue seas, and true Mediterranean sun. *Salammbo* sped at 6-8 knots to the southwest. The weather was favorable for filming, so I started to study the video camera I had received from the Delker company. I felt that there must be action in front of a video camera, and inspired by a misbegotten idea, I put the camera into Peter's hands. To create a spectacular scene, I jumped into the water holding on to a line fixed to the boat. On Lake Balaton, it is a favorite (though illegal) way of bathing to be towed by a boat on a rope. I don't mean to boast, but I had never before been unable to pull myself back to the boat. As soon as I hit the water of the Adriatic, I immediately felt that unusual speed and forces were at play. Knowing the limited maneuverability of the boat and yelling between gulps of water, I urged Peter to winch in the line. He did not hear me, and when I felt that my arms had stretched long enough, I had to let the line go.

Lightened by my departure, *Salammbo* jumped ahead and became smaller and smaller in the wave troughs. In a moment I was alone. The temperature of the water was pleasant, but I could not enjoy the seemingly long swim. The cause of my uneasiness was not antagonism to water, but to the possibility of sharks. I must confess that I am afraid of sharks. Though I tried diving in my seagoing years, I would only do so with a snorkel in a group dive. There is no sea without sharks. Following the refuse jettisoned from ships, sharks travel to the farthest reaches of the oceans. I also remembered times in the past when we had tied up in Monopoly, not very far from our present location, where sizable sharks were sometimes found in the fishermen's nets. For this reason I avoided long swims in the ocean.

I recalled one of the exceptions. My wife had accompanied me on one of my MAHART trips to the Far East on the ship *Petöfi*.[14] One day when we were at port in Tanga Bay in Tanzania, my wife went out windsurfing while I helped load the ship. The wide open bay faced the Indian Ocean. Fortunately I had been facing that way too, and I saw that my wife was struggling against the current of the outgoing tide. I immediately dove in and swam to help her, without even giving a thought to sharks. It was one of my longest sea swims, and pretty exhausting, but I was able to reach my wife and sail her safely back in. Our own fears quickly slip away when someone we care about is in danger.

Back in the Mediterranean the wind had increased to 6-7 on the Beaufort scale, and I felt more and more anxious. At last Peter struck the jib, pulled in the spinnaker's whisker pole so he could circle back against the wind, and started to tack back to me. A few minutes later we celebrated our reunion with Unicum. So, thanks to God, we can get to the moral of the story: the wind, just like distances, can be easily underestimated on the sea, and it is irresponsible to leave it out of our consideration.

Seamen are superstitious. They don't start out on Fridays, and they wait impatiently for the appearance of dolphins, the harbingers of good luck. All is well that ends well. In the golden rays of the dipping sun, a pod of dolphins approached the boat. They let us know with their spirited dance that we were welcome guests in Neptune's realm.

On the 26th of June, we had a spectacular day crossing the Straits of Messina. To the left of us were the somber mountains of Sicily. The 15- to 18-mile-long strait narrows like a funnel to about 2 miles at its narrowest part. We tacked into the strait in a strengthening north-northwest wind. Ferry boats crossed around us, and we met other sailboats as well. In the narrowest part we spied two boats of a strange design. On its long slender body was a mast with no sail. Most unusual was the bowsprit, which equaled the length of the body. Both boats had sentries on board. At first, we thought these craft to be research vessels. Later we found out that it was swordfish season, and the vessels were specialized fishing boats.

Nearing Scylla and Charybdis, we neither tied ourselves to the mast, nor plugged our ears with wax. But to be careful, we started the motor. In the section of the fastest current, whirlpools stirred up the surface of the deep blue water. The undertow changed *Salammbo*'s course and rolled the boat considerably. In the rushing, eddying currents, the multitude of fishing boats indicated the abundance of fish.

Because of the persistent calm, we sailed for nearly two days in the

---

[14] The opportunity to bring a spouse along was a privilege afforded only to MAHART employees who had been with the company for over five years.

vicinity of Sicily, trying to avoid the many fishing boats. One night a searchlight was aimed at us. When we were within hearing distance, they asked us to follow them. First we took them to be some kind of Mafiosi, but they were only guiding us to avoid their fishing nets (resulting in a 1.5 hour detour). Only after we had wished each other bon-voyage, I re-stowed the flare gun.[15]

On the 30th of June, we reached the shores of Sardinia. In a freshening breeze, *Salammbo* increased pace like a horse sensing its stable. We entered Cagliari harbor in the early afternoon, with salt-bitten but happy faces.

MY FLOWERY CONSOLATION

We tied the boat at an empty slip of the yacht harbor and started with unsteady steps on an exploratory walk. In the old city built on a hillside, the target of our expedition could only have been a bar with beer.

Stepping out of the marina gates, we heard the familiar cheer of fans: "Jozsi, add keresztbe" ("Joe, pass it along," in Hungarian). We followed the voices to an outdoor swimming pool. After fetching cold beers, we took our places among the fans. As the water polo game neared its end, we found out that only the coach of the visiting team, Kalman, and one of the players, Jozsef Domsodi, were Hungarians. Seeing our tanned hides, they invited us to use the showers, and to join them afterwards at a restaurant. Since they were running late for the airport, they hurried through their meal, but they still took time to see our boat before departing.

We had no time for further relaxation. Peter Szabó had to return to Hungary, and we had only three days for the two-man work. We set about fixing the problems that had popped up during the last leg of the journey. I serviced the motor completely. The standpipe of the cooling system received an extension pipe into the bilge, because the motion of the boat had caused water to spill on the alternator and electrical connections. The standing rigging needed looking at, and I tightened the stays to give the mast a definite bend. All of this work occupied us from morning to evening.

After the daily chores, we ate our dinner in the restaurant where we had gotten to know the polo players. I gave my wife the number of the pizzeria, so that I could hear the voice of my family daily. My friend Peter did not like those calls, because I became morose, silent, and unpleasant company afterward. Those conversations wore me down emotionally. The ever-lengthening calls were curtailed only by thoughts of the phone bills.

---

[15] Though designed to fire flares into the air as a distress signal, a flare gun like the Very pistol I had on board *Salammbo* is a lethal weapon if fired at close range—the knowledge of which would prove important to me more than once.

Above: *Bird's-eye view of Salammbo from the masthead.*

Back at the boat, we met the Sardinian agent of the local office of MAHART. With his help we got past the local formalities in good time. My employers had offered to cover the local expenses, so I made up a new list of purchases.[16] The time flew by, and before long the day came when Peter also flew. I sent my daughter chocolate, a world map, and a clock showing ship time. After our breakfast in the airport terminal, Peter went up to the departure lounge, and I to the restroom to hide my tears. A sailor about to embark on a circumnavigation should not show up with moist eyes. I felt rotten, and I was craving for the company of some living thing, so I took a bus to a store in the city. I returned to the harbor carrying a pot of flowers, and in a much better mood.

The next day the chandler arrived with the new equipment we had

---

[16] I was still an employee of MAHART at the time. I requested a one-year unpaid vacation in order to go on my circumnavigation, and MAHART signed on as one of my sponsors.

ordered. It took all morning to get everything from his car to the boat. I had to find safe and well-balanced storage on *Salammbo* for 250 one-liter bottles of mineral water, 16 liters of wine, 5 kilograms of onions, 1 kilogram of garlic, 10 kilograms of apples, and 3 kilograms of lemons. I also got a gas lighter, fuses for the radio, and anti-skid adhesive tape. The captain of the schooner in Bari had mentioned to me the danger of slipping on the companionway steps, and I wanted to eliminate this potential source of an accident.

The telephone discussion that evening with my wife Zsuzsa again troubled me, and I decided to depart the next day regardless of the weather. In the morning, MAHART's local representative, Anthony, waved a telegram when he came to bid me farewell. It was from the Equator Sport Club—Jozsef Gal wished me luck on the coming voyage in the name of the members. I hoisted the sails and forgot the previous evening's mood.

"THE LORD WAS MY GUIDE"

According to our plans we had worked out earlier in detail, I needed to head to the Balearic Islands in order to reach Gibraltar as early as possible. The continuation of the trip was as bad as the beginning. A stormy wind drove *Salammbo* as I left Cagliari on the first night. The extraordinarily unpleasant motion wore me down. I was seasick and cold. My bad temper was also fueled by some troubles on deck. The leech of the reefed main was not held fast by the reefing line stopper, which abraded the line as well. Despite the new waterproofing, the water came in through the porthole frames. The lee cloth of the bunk was uncomfortable, and in bigger waves I flew over it. The water in the tank under my bunk made loud splashing noises. I had to wrestle with the gas range just to cook some soup.

In the following days, the wind abated but the waves remained just as high. I deviated from the planned route by 60 miles. I was still plagued by seasickness, so it was a great achievement when I could cook a chicken soup, and an even greater one when it stayed in me.

Thanks to my instruments I started to feel like I was in an enchanted castle. The electrical supply voltage suddenly dropped below 11 volts. Then the speedometer[17] just switched off. The so far inoperative wind speed meter started to work. After I started the motor all the instruments kicked in again. A short while later, they successively stopped and started working.

I had already suffered endless problems with the depth sounder, but my hopeless struggle with the boat's electrical equipment really started from this day. The reason for this was that the greater part of my electronic equipment was obtained at the last minute, thanks to the generosity of my

---

[17] I have chosen to use the term "speedometer," though it is sometimes called a "knot meter."

sponsor. It would have been important to ground all the equipment, but that step was omitted. I would find out that I had too many consuming devices, or conversely, not enough energy.

When the weather permitted, I licked my wounds. After a few days I could wash myself, clean the dishes, and restore order in the cabin. The wind had been too weak for the wind vane, so I motored for eight hours to return to the planned route. One of my pleasures was that I had succeeded in cooking a Szeged-style fish soup from a can. Hungarians have a saying that the fish wants to swim again, so I let the carp from the Tisza River swim in Sardinian wine.

At the prearranged time I contacted the amateur radio station of the Equator Club in Szekesfehervar. Zsolt Pal told me the news that Nandor Fa had also started his voyage. Nandor had to hurry to reach the starting point of the BOC Around the World Single-handed Race in Newport. If everything went well, we should meet in Gibraltar.

On the 10th of July, the sea became stormy again, and trouble started immediately. I took down the Genoa in time, but my main crashed down.[18] The headboard came out.[19] I was still out laboring on the deck at midnight, when in the distance I spotted the lights of the island of Mallorca.

At 3:00 in the morning, I decided on a hazardous move upon reaching Porto Colom. In the pitch-dark moonless night, I sailed into the rocky harbor without a chart or a working depth sounder. I could see the narrow curving corridor only by the blinking, blinding glare of the lighthouse. They were exciting moments. In the perfectly protected bay, only the lapping of the sea could be heard. Enjoying the much desired quiet, I anchored between two resting yachts.

Luckily, despite my exhaustion, my senses registered the increasing wind and alarmed me. It was just in time, because the boat had started to drag. My smallish Bruce anchor had not held, and I was headed toward the stony banks of the bay. Quickly starting the motor, I returned to my originally selected place. I dropped a new anchor on 50 feet of chain and 120 feet of line, putting *Salammbo* under control once again.

At daybreak, a good breakfast was followed by a washing and tidying of the boat before I went to look around the fetchingly beautiful inlet. The sandy beach at the foot of steep rocky hills was to the liking of others too; a dozen yachts were anchored in the bay. The time for admiration had to end because I needed to put on a gymnastic production. It took several hours to fix *Salammbo*'s broken main halyard on the top of the 38-foot mast. This

---

[18] "Genoa" refers to a certain type of jib sail.

[19] "Headboard" in this context refers to a plate at the upper corner (or "head") of the mainsail, by which the sail is attached to the shackle of the main halyard.

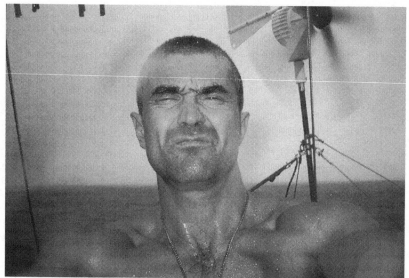

Above: *A salty self-portrait. The wind generator is visible behind me.*

was a good excuse for a swim, and I checked the underwater parts of the ship.

The next morning, I left the anchorage in ideal winds. Only then, in the light of dawn, could I see that the Lord had been my guide when I was going in among the hazardous rocks in the darkness.

In the following days, the southerly wind from Africa brought searing hot weather. During the night, the shrill alarm of the radar detector woke me several times; shipping traffic was increasing. Just as disturbing was the noise of the slapping sails in the waves. The radio fuse burnt out a second time. I tried to restore my balance by bathing and washing my hair.

I crossed the Greenwich Meridian on July 14. Not much later I had tense moments as *Salammbo* sailed over a 2-meter-deep bank. The boat's draft is 1.90 meters; it had been a close call. Leaving Cabo Palos behind me, I followed the Spanish coast. Unfriendly rainclouds gathered above the high and rocky outcrops, and the increasing thunder prompted me to reef the sails. I sailed into the Gulf of Cartagena for some filming. There are grandiose forts on the shores, for the bay is still a strategically important naval base. Before long I fled the harbor that evoked thoughts of menacing, macabre settings in stories.

Because of the increasing ship traffic and weak breezes, I slept on my feet for days. To prevent any accidents I sought a protected anchorage in the vicinity of Cartagena, behind the prominent Cape of Timos. At the end of the inlet, frighteningly close to the rocky shore, I dropped the anchor. Above me were several hundred meters of rock face, and a medieval fort hanging there like an eagle's nest gave me an ominous feeling. A bigger problem was that nothing protected me from the bashing of the waves, but since I was more afraid of hitting a ship, I stayed. I set the alarm clock hourly to check the anchor and the shore.

At dawn, I hoisted the sails to get away from that inhospitable place. The good run lasted until the next morning, and then the wind stopped. The waves, naturally, stayed to fray my nerves with the slapping sails. According to my log, I had slept only twice, forty minutes each time, in the last 24 hours. By the 18th of July, I had been underway alone for the tenth day in the Western Basin of the Mediterranean, under unfavorable circumstances. The dense traffic of ships and boats, the windless, swelling seas, and the increasing counter-current together allowed only minimal rest. It was a tremendous burden to sail under these conditions without an autopilot. In the afternoon another calm came up and I could not stand it anymore. I started the motor. At 1700 hours I saw Tariq's mountain… Gibraltar.

GOODBYE TO THE SHORES

The Rock, as it is called shortly and pointedly by the English, emerged as the culmination of my desires. I wanted to approach it directly by the shortest route, but all of a sudden I was stopped by standing waves. I fought them for a while before I recovered my senses and turned towards the Spanish shores. I knew, of course, that the strong currents peculiar to the Strait were caused by the tides of the Atlantic and the current of the higher salt content of the Mediterranean. It was a new experience to fight it with such a small boat. I entered the familiar harbor at sundown, with my strength ebbing. I still had enough energy to take some pictures of the atomic sub berthed there, but my enthusiastic photography session was ended by the objections of the white-clad marine guards. I asked directions of an incoming fishing boat and turned *Salammbo* towards the yacht harbor. Finally at 9:00pm I tied up at the designated slip in Marina Bay, quickly finished the paperwork with the officials, and was at last able to take it easy.

The marina's shower was closed, but the nearby restaurant was not. Not knowing what life may bring next, I ordered a great steak and, to make up for the shower, a beer. I noticed that the pants I was wearing, which had been just tight enough in Sardinia, had become quite loose. A later weighing confirmed it. I had lost 8 kg. (18 lb.) in 10 days. I swore that coming back, I would sail with a crew from Gibraltar. Would there be a voyage home?

The harbor and the city on the shores of the bay were old acquaintances. I had tied up here with the ships *Raba* and *Budapest* several times before. I had pleasant memories of Gibraltar, where British elegance mixed easily with Spanish lightheartedness on the streets. My first walk, though, was a grave disappointment. The city had become Africanized in

Above: *The official starting point of my solo, one-stop circumnavigation: the port of Gibraltar, July 1990.*

the worst sense. With its dirty streets, it gave an impression of disorder.

There was no time to be a tourist; I had to look after official matters. First I needed to meet with MAHART's local representative Richard. The endearing young man always addressed me as "Captain." I gradually got used to the courtesy title bestowed on me. Anything I needed would come from MAHART with Richard's help. However, answers were late in coming from MAHART, I still had not received the money I needed, and I had to act quickly.

In the harbor a small shop had a notice board where anything could be advertised for a small fee. In that nautical flea market, boats, journeys, crews offering their services for hire, charts, and equipment were all offered for sale. Desperate for cash, I entered the army of advertisers with a heavy heart. My notice had the details of my spare radio, and in capital letters, "FOR SALE."

I returned to the boat to start my work on deck. After 2,000 miles a lot had to be fixed. Before long, I was roused from my labors by a shout. A short, stout man in shorts called down to me between puffs on his pipe. Because of the low tide, my boat was positioned far below the dock. When I beckoned for my visitor, I saw immediately that he was in the caste of a true sailor, as he effortlessly jumped all the way down onto *Salammbo*'s deck with an agility that belied his age and stature. The introduction revealed that my guest, Mr. Werner, was a Danish physician who had cruised the seas with his wife for years. The visit was about my advertisement. Werner liked the set, and we agreed on the price quickly. But then the matter took an unexpected turn. When he learned of the enterprise for which I was preparing, he pushed away the set and gave me a lecture about the dangers to be encountered, emphasizing the importance of having a spare set. I had never before found a buyer who could argue so convincingly against the deal. His arguments ultimately won. I got no money, but I had gained a friend. And to prove that there are no coincidences but still some miracles, in the evening I got the telegram from MAHART promising financial support.

After this, my new friend Werner did not move from my side, except to busy himself with taking care of some of my affairs. Utilizing his many years of sailing experience, we methodically inspected the weak points of the boat, trying to find potential sources of danger. When I had finished with some repairs, Werner arrived with a new battery and wind generator. Following his advice, I also bought a better sextant, storm anchor, and other necessary spares.

It seemed that we would never get to the end of our labors. But one thing was never omitted from our daily routine: the five o'clock tea on Werner's beautiful yacht. This ceremony was conducted by my new friend's wife, who was as expert at tea making as at ocean sailing. Werner presented more and more new ideas. He tried to persuade me to interrupt my voyage in Australia, and start a race on the Pacific on a new boat, now anchored in New Zealand. I withstood his persuasions successfully, and he had to accept that this business would not be consummated.

On the evening of July 27, *Alba Regia* entered the harbor with Nandor Fa and his friends on board. I learned that this was his second day in the harbor, but somehow we had passed each other coming and going. We enjoyed it so much better when we were finally able to shake hands. It was a rare moment in the history of Hungarian sailing sport: two Hungarian boats were to start their circumnavigation from the same harbor.

Nandi was not in very good shape; the twenty-day Mediterranean voyage had also frayed his nerves. He was in a hurry, for he had to get across the ocean to Newport to start his singlehanded race.[20] I was in the greater hurry, planning my departure for the same day. But the weather decided otherwise. Stormy headwinds churned the bay's waters. We went to the city on our errands, and since the wind had not changed, we went back to the harbor only towards evening.

The people on the streets milled around us. The shops and restaurants were open. Our choice was a little pub on the waterfront. Inside, noisy

---

[20] The 1990-91 BOC Challenge was a singlehanded race around the world, starting and ending in Newport, Rhode Island. The race included stops in Cape Town, Sydney, and Punta del Este.

patrons made merry. The scene reminded us of one described by Jeno Rejto, one of our favorite writers.[21] We had chosen a pleasant spot, a step from the bay, under the open sky. The wind abated and the night became quiet. Looking around we saw the bobbing masts of hundreds of sailboats, and here and there the lights of the signs of businesses and restaurants. But we did not care as much for the sights as for each other's stories. While the waitress supplied pitchers of beer, we related our harrowing Mediterranean experiences. We each assigned choice adjectives to the sailor-plaguing standing waves and unpredictable mixed winds. Then, cutting into each other's words, we recounted the lighter events. It was good to discuss those as well.

It was exactly 11:00pm when I felt a change around me. The wind had sprung up in the late evening and turned fair. "Well then, I'll go now," I said to the company. And in a minute, with Nandi and his friends, I was hurrying to the boat. The goodbye had been simple, like at home when leaving a restaurant after having beer and pretzels.

Nandi released *Salammbo*'s lines from the shore and I disembarked. I had hoped to get out in the dark without much of a to-do, but I couldn't fool the vigilant Danish sailors with my silent routine. The well-wishes sounded from boat to boat, giving me frequencies and times, in the hope of contacting me later on in the faraway oceans. The strait's dark waters eddied in front of *Salammbo*. Astern, Nandi and his friends still waved from the end of the pier. I had started on my solitary trip around the world.

---

[21] Jeno Rejto was a Hungarian writer whose works have become famous even outside of his home country. He had a gift for writing very exciting and humorous stories. I had a special admiration for his work, which proved especially useful in pulling me out of the occasional bouts of depression that can descend upon the single-hander at sea.

3

TOWARD THE ZERO-DEGREE LATITUDE
(1990 July 28 — August 29)

"After all a man can't only do what he has to do, with what he has to do it with, with what he has learned, to the best of his judgement. And I reckon a hog is still a hog, no matter what it looks like."

—William Faulkner, *The Old Man*

THE WIND HUNG ONTO THE SAILS AS *SALAMMBO* DUG deeply into the waves and, shaking off the spray, heaved over the crests again. It blew from the north, and I hoped that it would last until I sailed through the critical part. I tried to spot the lights of both small and large vessels from the cockpit; I did not want to get in the way of any of them. The Strait of Gibraltar is 8 to 24 miles wide, and for a small sailboat it is like Broadway for a pedestrian—you have to fend for yourself when crossing it. Tankers, liners, and fishing vessels cross from the Mediterranean to the Atlantic and back in the narrow seaway. And the very strong currents make it even more hazardous for the sailor.

Tired from hand-steering all night, I only had time in the morning to jot down in the log the official departure time and date of my one-stop circumnavigation: July 28, 1990, 2330 hours. It was a simple entry, with scribbled letters and numbers just like any other data. Nothing special. I did not think of writing a fully capitalized note: "NOW IT BEGINS!" I was not thinking of the limitless distances, the unimaginable dimensions and spans of time. I was not considering how after the Strait, the Atlantic

47

swirled before me with its unfathomable 100 million square-kilometer size. Or that Hungary could fit into the Indian Ocean 800 times. Or that the next and only stop, in Australia, was more than four months away. But the clock had started; everything was now going for real.

ALONE FOR A YEAR

In the cabin, I guarded one book like a treasure: the story of the adventurous circumnavigation by the *Spray*, written by the Canadian captain Joshua Slocum. The first singlehanded long distance cruiser finished his voyage in 1898 on a boat he had personally restored. The date was significant. Although sailing is nearly contemporary with civilization, solo circumnavigation was not yet a century old when I embarked on my own journey in 1990. According to the records, the number of non-racing singlehanded circumnavigators up to 1989 was only 91. Ocean racers cannot be compared with the others. Their accomplishments are not less significant, but different, since they have support teams and resources such as organized tracking and rescue service available all along the way. Those who do it on their own are usually on smaller, less well-equipped boats, and have to rely mostly on their own mental and material resources. The nearly 100 non-racers who had done it over the 92-year span had done it in nearly 100 different ways. Because of the differences in their circumstances and the advances in technology of boat building and navigation, it is impossible to quantitatively compare and grade their achievements.

The route may be planned between the Tropics of Cancer and Capricorn using the Panama and Suez Canals, using the less dangerous equatorial zones. However, it is much faster to cross the more dangerous Southern Oceans. Important considerations regarding the choice of route are the direction of the circumnavigation, the size of the boat, and the equipment available. It is generally agreed that the most difficult route is the one around the five Capes: Cape of Good Hope, Cape Leeuwin, Southeast Cape, Southwest Cape, and Cape Horn. This way is both the fastest and the most dangerous. To qualify a route as "circumnavigation," the sailor has to cross two exactly opposite points on the globe (equal but opposite latitudes and 180° longitude difference). To evaluate the effort, one has to consider the number of stops, timing, and route direction. Taking all of the variables into account, I would rate my own enterprise at about 25th on the list of 91 in terms of difficulty—the boat size in the 5th place, and the equipment even higher... if I survived it.

My intention was to sail *Salammbo* around the five Capes within a year, so I had to give up the optimum timing of some sections. The basic reason for this was the speed limitation of a boat as small as mine. *Salammbo* is a displacement type boat, and as a cruiser, it has a short waterline even for a 31-footer. I had to accept that its speed could not normally exceed 4-5 knots, and its daily run would not be over 100-120 nautical miles. Knowing the distance and estimating the speed, I figured that some critical storm zones and dangerous areas would have to be crossed in the less than optimal season.

My plan therefore required compromises. I timed the Cape of Good Hope and Indian Oceans—which may be less dangerous—for the offseason, hoping that my sacrifice would pay its dividends on the Pacific. My plans were known before I started, and I received some criticism for them. My advisors could have been misled by the different timings of the great around-the-globe races. The starts of those races are timed according to the stops, rest periods, sponsors' requirements, and weather patterns, to ensure that the participants can expect the best conditions possible in each of the different stages. The participants in the major races have a minimum boat length of 50-60 feet. Their size and equipment (and the go-for-broke manner in which they are driven) enables them to have at least double *Salammbo*'s speed.

The route of a sailboat is determined by the global wind and ocean current systems. The charts accurately indicate the location of the Atlantic Trade Winds and the Westerlies on the Indian and Pacific Oceans. Many other details influence the choice: islands, shallows, capes, commercial sailing routes, icebergs, and depths. The potential difficulties include colliding with whales, and thousands of other problems. I had to be sure of one thing—that I would prevail!

WAVE-RIDING WITH STOMACH PAINS

Salammbo quickly noticed the long rolling waves of the Atlantic, which caused such a different motion than the Mediterranean. In the bright, hot sun and fresh breeze, the sailing was ideal. When heading for the Canaries, one needs only to sit on the Northeast Trades and ride on the fair Canary current, and everything should go without a hitch.

The Trade Wind driving *Salammbo* had been a trusted source of energy for the early navigators. In the northern hemisphere, air currents flow towards the Equator from the north. The turning motion of the globe (the Coriolis Effect) changes the direction of flow to northeasterly. In the southern hemisphere the wind direction is changed to southeasterly.

To adapt herself to the wind, *Salammbo* used twin jibs set on whisker poles. It looked like a butterfly. The doubled front stay came into play at those times. It made it possible to hoist two jibs at the same time. The number 3 jib (200 square feet) or the number 4 jib (120 square feet) were a good match for the wind strength, which I estimated at about 5-7 (Beaufort).

I had been troubled by a stomach problem for a few days, but the only thing that really concerned me was the wind vane. The yawing of the boat

Above: *A series of sailing variations on the Atlantic Ocean...*
First, sailing downwind with a so-called "wing-to-wing" arrangement, which requires having two sails of identical size, each supported by a spinnaker boom on either side, to balance the boat and ease the steering.

Above: *This is a unique point of sail between directly downwind and broad reach. There is still one spinnaker pole on the port side, but the starboard jib is more broad reach trimmed to stabilize this "mixed" point of sail.*

Above: *This is the traditional downwind sailing arrangement, with the main sail fully raised, where more steering is needed due to the unbalanced sail layout. This photo was taken somewhere between the Canaries and the Equator, heading towards the Cape Verde Islands.*

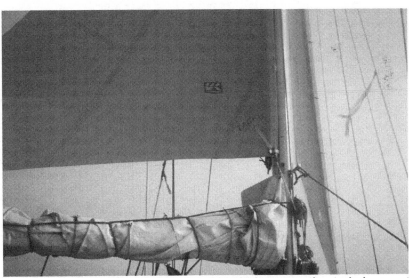

Above: *This photo depicts storm sailing, with only the storm sails raised: the storm jib and trysail. The jib is trimmed tight in the center of the boat to prevent broaching, and the trysail is used as a head sail with two sheets skipping the main boom, which presents the biggest danger in the event of an accidental jibe.*

Above: *The centered storm jib in this photo keeps the bow downwind and works as a broach preventer. The point of sail shown here is close to downwind. This photo was taken somewhere in the Roaring Forties, en route to Australia.*

reached 30-40°. The vane of the steering mechanism produces a correcting action, which is transmitted to the wheel by lines and blocks. In a following wind, the apparent wind speed (the difference between the true wind and boat speed) is low, and it affects the efficiency of the wind vane unit, even with a balanced sail plan. The difference between the wind direction and wave direction causes a deviation from the set direction. There are two possible remedies for this: hand steering or autopilot. My strapped finances had not permitted me to buy an autopilot or the means to produce electricity for it. I was left with the painful alternative: I had to steer as long as I had the strength to do so. The loss of distance gained aggravated me. It gave me no chance to better the sailing time of other similar sized boats when sailing downwind.

I tried a few tricks. Leaving the directly downwind course, I sailed on broad reaches.[22] I hoped this would result in better steering and a higher speed, causing a net gain in the VMG (velocity made good towards the target). I left one of the jibs, pulled in the whisker pole of the other, and

---

[22] "Running," or sailing downwind with the wind coming from directly behind, is generally slower than sailing at the other points of sail (such as broad reaches). Usually the sail acts under the influence of lift, since the air takes longer to travel over the leeward side of the sail than the windward side (much like the design of an airplane wing). On the contrary, while running, the sail is simply acting as a "parachute" of sorts, being pushed from behind by the wind. This is not only slower, but also makes it difficult to properly balance the wind vane.

trimmed in the sail. The boat speed and the apparent wind both increased, and the steering stabilized. Another solution I pursued was to rig a 60-square-foot sail to the backstay and sheet it to the mast in the centerline. The sail acted as a vertical stabilizer, reducing the swinging of the stern. My daily averages increased, but I could not solve the problem completely. Unfortunately, I had to give up any further experimentation because of my worsening health.

My stomach was still troubling me. After the exertions in the Mediterranean, I had arrived in Gibraltar with a 20-pound weight loss. As a seaman, my regular weight had been 200 pounds. After becoming a deck officer, with less physical work, I had held my weight to 180 pounds. The weighing in Gibraltar had terrified me. It reminded me of the story of the famous circumnavigator, Francis Chichester. He was almost unable to complete his one-stop voyage because of the catastrophic decline of his body weight. With this in mind when I was in Gibraltar, I had forced down puddings with whipped cream, and lots of ice cold beers. My weight increased, but at the same time I succeeded in getting an inflammation of the bowels. I did not return to my senses in time, and the unnecessary overeating of my perishable foods (to prevent spoiling) had only aggravated the situation.

On the 2nd of August I noted my painful symptoms in the log. In the evening I made contact again with the Equator station and listed my complaints to Zsolt Pal. Zsolt knew what to do, and connected me through the airwaves with his old ham pal, Feri. A friendly voice came on, as it turned out, from Dusseldorf. Feri is a surgeon in the clinic in Bottrop. According to my complaints, he tried to diagnose the malady and advised which medications to fish out of my first aid kit. Feri gave his phone number to Zsolt so we could reach him on the radio in case anything happened. I swallowed the pills Feri had recommended and I felt better— probably from the knowledge that somewhere in a distant land, there were people who thought and cared about me.

THE HAZARDS OF FREEDOM

I was lying in my bunk, if you can call the constant rolling lying. If there was one thing I hated, it was my own weakness, and now the usually friendly and protective cabin felt like a cage. My illness mainly bothered me because of how it limited my freedom. My thoughts concentrated on it. Freedom for me is one of the most important ingredients of a happy and balanced life, along with learning and observing. In the areas of our knowledge and experience we can move with confidence, gaining the assurance that is equally as important as freedom.

As I lay trapped in my sickbed I was voyaging back in time, landlocked as a sailor. In early 1984 I had been troubled by similar thoughts of

Above: *My friends at the Equator Station were my lifeline and a constant source of support.*

confinement, and it had prompted me to make a decision that was hard for others to understand. As a Merchant Marine officer, with my diploma in my pocket, I applied for the job of harbormaster in Balatonalmadi. When the director of MAHART's shipping branch for Lake Balaton questioned why I would apply to a job for which I was so grossly overqualified, I claimed to him that my fondest wish was to bike up to the end of the pier and, in front of the intently watching kids, ceremonially fire the color-coded storm flares.[23] My would-be director eyed me suspiciously, but he had to admit that my qualifications for the position were certainly sufficient. As one more feather in my cap, into my records went the title of Harbormaster. My family and friends still could not understand my motives for this new move. They could not appreciate that I would go backwards on the social ladder for the sake of my political independence and love for navigation, even in a shore position.

The pier and its surroundings represented for me a place of freedom and the realization of my fondest ideas. I was full of energy. I rented the plot of land beside the lake and started to build a yacht harbor. My family enterprise—Vizenjarók G.M. (Seagoing G.M.) was the first private enterprise in the country to render service to sailors. Lacking both capital and credit, I worked extremely hard to implement this novel idea. My diploma from the College of Physical Education merely gave me a permit to

---

[23] The storm notification system on Lake Balaton at the time consisted of firing a red flare to warn of an impending storm, or a yellow flare in the case of what would be comparable to a small craft advisory in the U.S. Today's modern system utilizes flashing lights rather than flares.

teach sailing; the actual art of instruction had to be obtained through practice. I poured the profits of my work-filled seasons right back into the development of the marina and boats. I had to do that because the worsening economic climate had compelled many of the state-owned clubs and institutions on Lake Balaton to open their facilities to the public. In other words, they had followed my example and were now giving me competition.

Above: *My very first sailing students, Lake Balaton 1984.*

In the meantime, both to avoid the mental numbing of repetitive work and in preparation for the expected political changes, I earned a second diploma from the Foreign Trade College. This assured my position with MAHART, and I was duly awarded the magnificent raise of 400 forint per month (about $2.00 in USD) for my foreign language qualification.

My studies and ideas for promoting tourism and the future of Lake Balaton were nevertheless sunk. More accurately, they did not disappear, but appeared under somebody else's name. I saw few of my own plans succeed. After some soul-searching I got over the second generation loyalty (my father had worked for MAHART for 50 years) and I took my personal enterprise out of the company.

To achieve my far-fetched dreams of developing a modern yacht harbor, I had to look for an out-of-country partner, and I found one. But the timing of our joint venture could not have been worse. The realization of our plans coincided with a growing official discrimination against such enterprises and a stifling of individual initiatives. It was a great disadvantage to be in the county of Veszprem. The county has a strategic position, and its "appointed" leaders were expected to be loyal to the Party line. This loyalty was the only prerequisite for any office. The anti-free enterprise sentiment found itself a secure place. The gauntlet was thrown. Accusations, intrigues, the stifling of individual ambitions... it was all reminiscent of the lawless time of the 1950's. Accusers could be easily found, but law and justice could not. A shady investigation was launched, our phones were tapped, our cars were followed... At the height of our troubles, my Austrian business partner was arrested. We faced a nasty uphill legal battle. In the end, we came out clean, but our business was completely ruined in the process.

I came to a crossroads. If I could not finish what I had started, how could I continue my life? On my checkpoints in life my tests were rated highly, but my diligently built roads were now plowed over. Should I trudge along anyway, and if the ditches became chasms, would I fall with those who joined me and had faith in me? Or was I judging myself wrong? Was it possible that despite appearances I was not a survivor? These are the questions for which each man tries to find answers.

I knew that if I could not answer these questions, then I might stray from my path. For me, the deviation from the socially acceptable patterns was not something like the temptation of alcohol. I felt that I could diverge from my own norms to become an entrepreneur like a shopkeeper or gas station operator, or anything else that had nothing to do with sailing or the maritime business. But these would have meant losing the values of responsibility and loyalty to my country.[24]

In that time of self-doubt, one thought flashed into my mind like a dream from my childhood: sail solo around the world in my own sailboat. According to maritime law, I would be taking a part of Hungary with me. It would be a revaluation, a unique chance for me to rearrange my priorities. Losing my business proved to be a major motivating factor in pushing me towards this endeavor. I was tired of being punished by society in spite of doing nothing wrong. I needed to place myself in the one arena in which my efforts could be fairly and objectively tested. To circumnavigate with only one stop was a sufficiently difficult challenge. It would be at the same time both a professional and patriotic undertaking.

My plan took shape, but it was difficult to allay my uncertainty. This

---

[24] The growth of private enterprise in Hungary started with entrepreneurs having the opportunity to rent state-owned grocery stores or gas stations in what was still very much a government-controlled, state-owned economy. Many of these individuals cheated the system. Due to their corrupt business practices, the store and gas station owners were doing financially well. Financial stability was something I could enjoy, but the corruption that would be needed to achieve it was not.

doubt was rooted in my apprehension regarding the future of my family. My wife and my preteen daughter had already endured the fate of a seaman's family—the many separations, the long absences. But this undertaking was quite another thing entirely. Its dangers could not be compared with my other voyages. It also carried the possibility of failure, which in this case would mean the loss of a husband and father. I had to answer the question though. Would a person looking in vain for a meaning for his life on land not engender the same loss? I needed to prove to the world and to myself that there was nothing wrong with me, that I had the ability to achieve the goals for which I fought. I determined that I would create better opportunities for my life, and all of our lives, if I chanced it. I can never adequately express my gratitude to my family for understanding my thoughts and also accepting the challenge.

MY RIDE ON THE AIRWAVES TO THE HUNGARIAN CIRCLE

Salammbo, running with the Trades, reached the Canary Islands. What pleased me more was that my health had improved. After spending a long period of time crawling around in pain at the helm, I could finally stand with a straight back again. I would have enjoyed gazing at the mountain peaks of some of the islands, but other duties soon commanded my attention.

I noticed that the 5-gallon diesel can, kept in the cockpit, had sprung a leak. The 2-cylinder 18 HP Volvo Penta engine, from Csepel Auto, originally had a 50-Amp alternator. We had installed another alternator, which increased both the alternator capacity and the fuel consumption. For that reason, in addition to the 10-gallon built-in fuel tank, I put diesel into two flexible 12-gallon tanks and a 5-gallon plastic container. This made my fuel capacity 55 gallons. The can in need of repair was stowed in the only free space left, beside the helm.

To make the situation more difficult, the wind and sea became stormy. I cast anchor in the lee of the Cape of Punta De La Aldea on Gran Canaria. The Cape's rocky outcropping protected me somewhat from the wind and waves, and I was able to start repairing the plastic can in quiet.

After that came electrical repairs. The wire in the mast was short-circuiting, and none of my masthead lights worked. I was unable to repair that, as the mast would have to be pulled to get at the wire. Fortunately I was prepared to encounter such problems—I had the navigation lights on the pulpit's fore and aft.

These night repairs gave me no anxiety because I had purchased a useful headlamp in Gibraltar. This miner's lamp-like contraption served me well for reading the sextant and stopwatch during nightly celestial observations.[25] The log stopped working again and I could not find the source of the trouble.[26] But I wasn't worried; the Sat. Nav. still worked.

After finishing my chores, I weighed anchor in the midst of the relentless wind and waves. It proved to be a real fight. In the Force 8 wind I did not hoist the main, only the storm trysail. Even so I nearly straightened out my reluctant Bruce anchor. Not much later, I had to say goodbye to the cut off anchor. Running with the wind in open water, I left the wave-battered Cape behind. I had only one useful anchor left, and the next chandlery where I could buy a new one was 16,000 miles away. Because of the routing of my voyage, this gave me no concern at all; the anchor was only necessary during coastal navigation anyway.

EXCERPTS FROM THE LOG

August 7, 1990

There was a wonderful full moon. Unfortunately between 3:00 and 4:00 in the morning the wind stopped. In the morning I found a flying fish in the cockpit. After cleaning, it could not have been more than 10 decagrams (4 ounces), but it was very tasty. My health improved magically, and for the first time since Gibraltar, I did my exercises.

I was 150 n. miles from Africa. My heading was 212°, and a half-knot current was pushing me. For supper, I cooked liver dumpling soup with military wrangler meat and egg noodles. In addition to my own maintenance, I had to care for the boat. The rotating parts had to be lubricated, and the stainless steel sink was rusting in the seawater. There was no boat traffic. The African coast was very empty.

August 9, 1990

My daily run was only 90 n. mile, the temperature was 25° C (77° F), the wind speed Force 2 weak. During the night I had seen the mast lights of a steamer going north.

I felt again that not everything was in order in my stomach, so I went back to my diet. This meant condensed milk for morning tea and carbon pills 3-4 times a day.

I crossed the Tropic of Cancer and for dinner I had rice and water… I felt better. In the evening I joined the Hungarian circle via ham radio

---

[25] When I say "nightly," I am referring more specifically to the twilight period each evening. This was a good time to make celestial observations, as the stars, planets, and horizon were all reasonably visible (which would not be the case either in broad daylight or complete darkness).

[26] "Log" in this context refers to a tool (sometimes called a "chip log" or "ship log") that is used to measure the speed of a vessel at sea.

Above: *A flying fish arrives on board Salammbo just in time for breakfast.*

communication.[27] According to the regular program we met at 2100 hours UTC (Greenwich Mean Time). The Hungarian radio hams, from Hungary and abroad, waited patiently until I had related my message to the Equator station in Szekesfehervar. The company was very interesting. In addition to names from home, there were compatriots from Germany, the USA, Brazil, Argentina, and Uruguay. That evening PY2ZZA (Uncle Nandi from Sao Paulo) joined in, as well as GOFDI (András from London), and naturally DJ8EF (Feri, my physician from Dusseldorf).[28]

I prepared myself for the evening meeting. When the weather permitted, I scheduled my dinner so that I could participate in the Hungarian circle. Every time I sat down at the shortwave radio set, the whole world seemed to open up. I had spent a lot of time as a radio officer aboard ships, but the official radio protocol permitted only the exchange of necessary information between ships or ship and shore. It was amusing to listen to the conversational tone of the amateurs.

Introductions, a round of answers to the always curious questions… it was a good feeling to talk to the whole world from my enclosure. It felt like

---

[27] I use the term "Hungarian Circle" to describe the various Hungarians scattered throughout different parts of the world who all joined together to stay in contact with me via radio communication throughout my journey.

[28] The capitalized alphanumeric combinations mentioned here are the respective ham radio call signs of my friends. Every licensed ham radio operator in the world has a completely unique call sign.

I was admitted to homes from Szekesfehervar to Brasília. I could picture the women watching TV in the next room, as old and young men alike tuned their sets to ask: "How are you, Istvan?"

I got to know their ages, occupations, and other information about their lives from my bobbing cabin. I knew that Gyuri from Sarawak, Borneo, got up early to check in and inquire about my condition. Then he would note with satisfaction that he was leaving to go to work.

The real lifeline was HA4EHQ, Zsolt and Karcsi from the Fehervar coast station. I couldn't possibly calculate how many nights they had spent, and would spend, in the Oreghegy building of the local telephone company[29] hunting for *Salammbo*. I knew that they were fanatics, and while they transmitted their call signs hundreds or thousands of times, they gave news about Hungary to the whole world. They were missionaries who carried the flag in their own way.

August 13, 1990

There were birds and even a butterfly flying around the boat, announcing the proximity of land. I didn't have to scrutinize the horizon for long before the barren mountains of the Cape Verde Islands came into sight. The wind and the current became weaker and changed direction. As the motion of the sea grew gentler, it permitted me to perform previously neglected chores. I made it a wash day, but I was not satisfied with the results. The laundry detergent I had bought in Bari dissolved in the seawater, as it was supposed to, but it had no cleaning action. My clothes dried in the intense sun, and I banged them together to shake out the dried salt. Strong winds can blow the salt off, but the beating is necessary in a calm. I had gotten used to my salty hair, but in the high humidity it became slushy. That was enough of that. I got out my scissors and razor, and within minutes I was bald. Immediately, tolerating the climate became easier.

August 15, 1990

I drifted slowly between the islands, fighting the disappearing breezes. After the brisk runs, the plodding was maddening. At 7:00 in the morning the radar detector alarm was activated by a 2,000-ton ship. I sailed near Brava, the southernmost island of the Cape Verdes. The Northeast Trades returned, giving me a pleasant 5-knot speed. After my morning milky grist, coffee, and cerbona slice (granola bar), my stomach felt good. I kept to 212° on a quarter wind, though in the last 24 hours, the wind had come from all directions. At 1400 hours UTC, I made a radio contact with Jozsi Gal. He was working hard on his new boat, but could always find time for

---

[29] The company's name in Hungarian is "HELYKOZI TAVBESZELO IGAZGATOSAG."

rag-chewing. After the chat, my mood was lifted by a pod of dolphins cavorting around the boat. I said goodbye to the sinking sun with a glass of brandy, and finished the day with a good tripe stew.

Above: *Harbingers of good luck: dolphins cavorting around Salammbo.*

August 16, 1990
In the morning I read the literature and prepared myself for the next stage. I strictly followed the advice of *Ocean Passages of the World*. The fat volume gives recommendations for shipping routes, based on many centuries of experience.

In the evening I got a surprise at the radio. I contacted one of the MAHART ships and talked to Karcsi Rajnai and my old colleague Adam Juhasz, alias Lemon. Lemon had learned of my trip from the TV, and was overjoyed to get in contact with me. Lemon is a disciplined radio operator; his well wishes were condensed into a few words.

For several days, I was the only one able to talk to Nandi Fa. The *Alba Regia* sailed on the North Atlantic towards America. Nandi had to report his position to the BOC race organizer, but his radio system had serious problems. Fortunately there was *Salammbo* to act as the missing link. Through these relays, the information reached Newport. The many hours of long transmissions helped to pass the time, but they used up energy as well. Because of the weak winds, the wind generator did not charge enough, and I had to run the motor.

August 20, 1990
The temperature was 26° C (79° F), the boat was healing 30-35°, and the

sea was rough. *Salammbo* sailed at about the latitude of Sierra Leone. In the morning I met two whales. They surfaced about 500 yards ahead of the boat, but I saw the column of their blows first. I didn't forget that the day was a holiday, Saint Stephen's Day. To celebrate the day of my namesake, I put on the tape of the Hungarian National Anthem. Then came the feast: a glass of brandy.

August 21, 1990

I had a great surprise when I left the cabin. Looking around, I saw a huge ship about a third of a mile away. The 30- to 40-thousand-ton ship was at least 600 feet long, the size of a small island. I could not understand why the radar detector had not alerted me. How could the tanker have gotten so close? I went down and called the ship on the VHF radio. We cleared it up quickly—the ship's radar was not operating. Happy in the knowledge that my detector was still working, we exchanged a friendly goodbye.

The boat's position, plotted on the chart, was nearing the Equator. I planned to cross 5° North Latitude at about 017-019° West Longitude. There I would turn and cross the Equator at around 024° West. My favorite afternoon entertainment was to watch the sun go down. In those parts the sun sets like it was yanked down. The sundown gives accurate clues to the next day's weather. If it is red, good weather is in store; if it is yellowish, stormy weather is to be expected.

The fish jumped by the dozens… feeding time of the predators. I like the fish, but not the fishing.

The temperature of the cabin was 28° C (82° F), but outside the wind cooled it to 23-25° C (73-77° F). Moderate seas were introducing the Doldrums. I caught myself becoming homesick. As a seaman I had never experienced homesickness; maybe I had become soft.

INSTEAD OF CALMS, MONSOON

The 5-6,000 miles sailed so far could be classified into four sections. The Mediterranean had greeted me with calms and variable winds, and the Northeast Trades had pushed the boat from Gibraltar to the Cape Verde Islands. From Brava Island to 9° North latitude, the winds changed around, and later the south-southwest winds blew. These last ones indicated irregular monsoons in the region—much rain in addition to strong winds.

On the 23rd of August it rained the whole day. I did not see the sun at all. In spite of the violent motion of the boat, I was able to catch 40 liters of rainwater. The bucket was fastened to the boom, and from there I transferred the salty, sandy water into bottles. It was good for washing myself. One bottle was enough for a whole bath.

The pouring rain squeezed me into the cabin and the boat moved savagely. Drinking water sloshed noisily despite the built-in baffles. I wrote in the log, "My nerves can hardly take it."

I tried to read books that would keep my spirits up. After Jack London's books, I read William Golding's *The Lord of the Flies*. I don't simply like this book; its message has a very special meaning for me. I read it again and again. The important matters for the marooned children were looking after the fire, cleaning themselves and their abodes, and maintaining their culture and structure. I felt that I had to guard the order and standards that tied me to civilization. I had to remain vigilant not to sink to primitive levels. To achieve this I needed to maintain a strict discipline. When I could do it, I shaved. I rigorously exercised. It improved my physical and mental condition. I ate from a plate rather than straight from the pot, though it was sometimes impossible because of the wave action. I listened often to the BBC broadcasts to try to get an idea of what was happening, no matter how far away it was. This was the way I guarded the fire on *Salammbo*.

I reached my planned turning point on the 25th of August and I changed tack. It was my practice that every time I changed tacks, which leads to the wind switching sides, I would restock everything movable to the windward side. This lessened the boat's heel, and increased its speed. The rearrangements were hard work, but they were worth it if the boat was on one tack for any length of time. I could re-ballast by changing the water from one side tank to the other with a set of valves.

I retuned the standing rigging because the monsoon virtually eliminated the calms of the Doldrums. The turn of weather was astonishing. Where I was counting on slow plodding, a Force 6-7 wind churned the oceans. The deck was continuously underwater, the boat heeled over 35°, and *Salammbo*'s dance on the bashing waves sometimes made writing completely impossible.

There were surprisingly many fish and fowl around the boat. I tried to identify the birds from a field guide.

During the daily radio connection we discussed my nutrition. The supplies had been arranged by the military, Major László Dán, and Judit Bataszeki. They had done it with their heart and soul. Opening the sealed packages often gave me very pleasant surprises. I anticipated them like Christmas packages. I related some of my experiences to them: "Don't send butter to Australia, it is inedible; the coffee and tea become lumpy." The next supply package should be for four months, not for six.

My breakfast that day was cereal with lemon juice, chicken sausages with cheese, garlic, and tea. For lunch, I warmed Temesvari slices from the military supplies. I had to force myself to eat, not because of the taste of the food, but because I was losing my appetite. It was not because of the motion of the boat; I just didn't feel well. In those days there was nothing I could enjoy. It was about 2 months since I had started to sail alone, and at that point it might have been caused by hypochondria. I had felt a sharp pain below my ribcage since Gibraltar, and it was getting worse. I was tortured by the notion that I had appendicitis, and I was afraid that it would perforate.

The sickness and solitude caused me to spot signs of depression in myself. I was standing at the helm and berating myself for the whole crazy idea of this undertaking. My anger was directed at the weather as well. It was 27° C (81° F) in the cabin, but outside in the wind, with breaking waves bathing the deck, it was much cooler. Only I could be so unlucky in the Doldrums. I had to fight a storm, and I was cold at the equator.

THE DIARY OF NEPTUNE'S DAUGHTER

On August 29 at 8:00 in the morning, I crossed the equator at 022°35' West Longitude. The sea was stormy—I crossed 0° Latitude in Force 5 winds. After the worries of the last few days I was not in a festive mood. To mark the event in some way, I tried to remember my previous crossings of the equator. I had crossed on the MS *Raba* going to Bombay, and on the *Petőfi* going from Tanzania to Singapore and on to Australia. This was my ninth crossing.

Then I remembered that my wife had once been with me. After serving five years with MAHART, seamen earned the privilege of bringing their spouses with them on the ship, if they chose. On many ships, it has long been a custom to host an elaborate and dramatic ceremony marking the "initiation" of passengers aboard who are crossing the equator for the first time. There are different roles for the various crew members, with Neptune—often played by the ship's captain—as the star of the show. The *Raba* had been no exception to this tradition. There was a shared souvenir from that trip that I carried with me—the book Zsuzsa wrote about the voyage.

Finding the chapter about the equator crossing, I forgot about the wind, the sea, and the waves smashing into the boat. This is what Neptune's daughter wrote about her initiation:

* * *

"The initiation will be today," the loudspeakers announced, "Tremble you mice, tremble you pagans." I am waiting to be snatched and to undergo different trials so that the god of the sea, Neptune, will make me a Christian from a pagan and a sailor.

I know that Istvan will be the physician; I sewed his costume. I hear the banging on the cabin door. Amidst victorious war cries I am bound by rogues wearing grass skirts and smeared with a mixture of cocoa and oil. Around their necks are chains of bones and they carry a whip and a lance.

Out of the waters of the swimming pool rises Neptune with a silver crown on his head, shaking his trident. In his tattered toga he is looking for the captain to accuse him of responsibility for the impossible conditions. He let pagans board the ship. The captain pacifies Neptune. To avoid sailing into a storm because of the pagans, he gives Neptune the 5-foot key of his country.

"God of Seas, do what you have to do," says the captain. Neptune calls the mermaid, astronomer, barber, physician, nurses, rogues, and pirates in fitting verses.

There is nothing to do; the pagans have to be baptized. The astronomer raises his beer bottle to the sky and inspects its bottom. He calls the pagans one after another, listing their sins. Before we can gain absolution and be baptized, we have to put our outsides and insides in order, and have to prove that we can cross the equator without outside help.

I am the fourth to be called before Neptune. I listen, on my knees, to the list of my sins. My transformation starts with the outside. I am put into stocks and my cleansing begins. My fashionable hairdresser tells me that blond is not in; black will suit me better. My braids are opened with a rake-like comb. Before dyeing, my hair is washed with ultra dishwasher liquid. To remove my wrinkles he applies paste to my face... good stuff, red and blue. My hairdresser, a donkeyman in civvies, knows how to apply grease, de-rusters, and other sprays. Then comes a pedicure and manicure. My mother could not identify me when my beauty finally satisfies the barber.

"What sickness could gnaw on you from inside?" asks my doctor. They tie me to the operating table with heavy chains. After a thorough examination they find that I have claustrophobia. The therapy starts right away. The doctor believes only in natural therapy and uses only noble organic stuff. In what way and order I cannot guess, because my eyes are full of some vile medicine. Out of the orgy of smells I can identify oil, honey, WD-40, and Camembert cheese. Since I take my medication bravely I am given, as a bonus, the feathers of a slit open pillow.

In my feathered state I stick and stink. The time comes when, all cleansed, I must prove that I can cross the 10-footlong, 2-footwide plank 'Equator' without help. Ropes fastened in zigzags and water hoses turned on from in front and back make the crossing difficult.

But I succeed!

All ragged, but proud, I can approach Neptune. To show my veneration I kiss the hand of his wife, the mermaid, smeared with stinky cheese. An egg is broken on my head, with which the mermaid shows that she accepts the fealty. I offer some drinks—three cases of beer—to Neptune, and then he baptizes me with ice cold water.

Above: *Photo from the extravagant Equator-Crossing Ceremony on board the M/V Petöfi, 1982.*

The last ceremony is to drink a toast with the captain and other baptized ones. I empty my glass of seawater. After the proceedings, songs, and laughter, Neptune and his servants give the key of the boat and return where they came from… the swimming pool.

* * *

I read Zsuzsa's writing a second time, and it made me smile again. I was thinking of inventing some ceremony for myself, but I couldn't think of anything other than to check my navigational calculations with "scientific accuracy." I pumped water into the sink and it drained out counterclockwise. Without a doubt, I was in the southern hemisphere.

4

THE STORM ZONE OF THE SOUTHERN OCEAN
(1990 August 30 — September 28)

"Every good book influenced the formation of my ideals and world concept, but every bad man helped to modify them."

—Rath Vegh Istvan

THE SOUTHERN ATLANTIC OCEAN RETURNED ME FROM my reverie soon enough. The wind and sea were rough. Gray 10- to 15-foot waves heaved the boat. Dark, depressing clouds raced across the sky. My only consolation was that *Salammbo* was progressing well. During one of the evening radio talks, I discussed the weather with Terike, the wife of Zsolt Pal. We agreed that the year's maximum sunspot activity helped not only radio communications, but also cyclonic activities. My daily averages proved this. On August 30 I traversed 130 nautical miles, despite the fact that I was still sailing in the Doldrums.

My supplies dwindled along with the miles. The 85-liter tank under my starboard bunk ran empty, and what was more depressing, so did my bottle of brandy. My repairs were extensive: I replaced a broken block on my wind vane with a new one, and the emptied bottle with a full one.

My ham radio friends gave me the news that Nandi Fa had arrived in Newport. High time, since I heard that he had suffered kidney cramps while underway.

I thought a lot about *Salammbo*'s resilience; I was amazed how she took the beatings of the ocean like a well-trained fighter. With the miles piling

67

up, it became my daily practice to make a brief excursion into the lands of fantasy. It was my mind's defense to guard against the monotony and the solitude. I could switch myself off from focusing on the surroundings while my senses still gathered and processed their information, and alerted me when necessary. My memory returned to *Salammbo*'s construction, which was when my trials had begun…

* * *

After I decided on the circumnavigation, the major part of my inheritance from my mother's estate covered the costs of starting to build the boat. The money was enough to buy the hull, deck, and cast-iron keel of a Balaton 31-foot sailboat from the Balatonfüred boatyard. I wanted to build the boat as cheaply as possible, but to the highest of standards. I was prepared to spend most of my time and energy on boatbuilding, but I would also need the services of experts.

It is difficult to find good and honest craftsmen in any field, but in building individual boats it is nearly impossible. Small boat construction is very demanding work, requiring multifaceted skills that can only be learned well over a period of decades. I trusted that I could find the last Mohican of this trade. I circled Balaton a few times in my search, but in vain. I complained about this to Uncle Pista Nemeth, the record holder of the Blue Ribbon Race, and like magic he mentioned a name. The name of Bruckner has a distinguished history. But its founder, Master Jani, like many distinguished veterans, limited himself to minor projects and repairs. Fortunately his nephew, Jozsi, was just building a workshop to start his own business. We understood each other immediately, and worked well as a team. Balogh Dezso joined us in our endeavor. He was a virtuoso master of stainless steel fabrication. I chose Zoltan Konkoly for the electrical work. For fiberglass and plastics, we found Gyula Egyed to be the expert. We were also joined by Sandor Deli, the diesel expert. I was the nautical expert, driver, painter, helper, and general busybody, including the demanding and annoying buyer within my circle of friends. All of us worked together on the various phases of boatbuilding.

The members of the team invested a huge amount of energy in the boat, not caring for their own wellbeing. Unlike Kelemen Kömuves in the fables, we did not wait for our walls to crumble, but instead took off anything not meeting our approval and started over from scratch when necessary.[30] We

---

[30] The allusion here is to a Hungarian folk ballad describing the construction of the famous Fortress of Deva in modern-day Romania. According to the legend, Kelemen Kömuves ("Clement the Mason") tried to build the fortress walls each day, only to find they had collapsed by the following morning. Ultimately he was able to build the fortress to last, but at a tragic price. In my case, I was willing to go through the pain of undoing our own work in order to ensure it was done properly.

worked and lived together like a family. We put down the tools late in the evening and trekked home 6-10 miles to Csopak or Almadi in the middle of the night, even in snow and sleet.

In building the boat, we concentrated on reliability, strength, and practicality. First we fastened the 1.5-ton keel to the hull. We made everything over-secure and from the best materials possible. Anticipating the aggressively corrosive and electrolytic effects of the sea, we made every metal part of stainless steel, bronze, or anodized aluminum. We installed sacrificial anodes at the meetings of different metals.

The boat was then brought to Jozsi Bruckner's workshop in Aracs and put on a stand. The deck was still in the shipyard in Füred, where we started on the reinforcements. In the yard they looked at me with more and more astonishment, like sympathetic teachers at an eager but clueless student, and they helped me a lot. Much of our work was focused on reinforcing the deck to make sure it was supported properly. A sailboat out at sea often endures tremendous forces of pressure coming from above. Working on the same shift as the regulars, we put girders (beams/stringers) on the ceiling below the deck, making the deck extraordinarily stiff. We put on oversized receptacles (counter plates) for the deck fittings and stanchion bases, which would distribute the load on the deck evenly to prevent damage. The deck openings were also made differently from the standard. Soon the deck was also transferred to the workshop in Aracs.

Above: *An "X-Ray" view of Salammbo's interior. The view of the "coffin bunk" in the lower left gives you some idea of how claustrophobic my sleeping quarters were.*

Where the deck joined smoothly to the hull, we fastened them together with epoxy and 300 stainless steel screws. For the next few weeks, I became the vole of the shipyard. Wearing a gas mask, I ground the inside of the hull amidst terrible dust and noise. We thought that the original thickness of the hull was inadequate, so we laid it up to double thickness under the waterline, counting on the possibility of hitting ice or another ship. We used a good part of the 550 kilograms of polyester resin and the quarter of a ton of fiberglass purchased for the job. We laminated the gunwale[31] from the inside and from the outside. We built crossbeams into the hull, as on the deck. *Salammbo* swallowed all of the materials, increasing the weight and draft, making her akin to a bomb shelter.

The steering was installed and soon the woodwork could start. We attached the deck fittings and bonded the keel. A key point was the proper rigging of the mast. Sometimes we worked on a project for a week, only to start all over if we were not satisfied with the results. We followed this practice any time we had any doubts. Jozsi's wonderful woodwork started to put some soul into the stark fiberglass interior. Everywhere there were nice curves instead of sharp corners. We doubled the interior furniture, which in addition to the regular purpose of storage, also served as a reinforcing grid framework to provide extra support for the hull. Contrary to the accepted practice, we did not trim the gunwale. It served as a good stiffener, and we looked for reinforcing rub rails too. Some boats use rub rails like handrail coverings.

I discovered that the firm Pemu produced some joint protectors for the shipyard and river police. Unfortunately, the time-consuming and energy-sapping factory visits did not bring any results. I could not find the required profile. I was ready to give up when, at the Dusseldorf Boat Show, I discovered a satisfactory Danish product. All I had to do was locate one of my acquaintances living in Denmark, and soon we were cooking the 200-pound stuff in a barrel. A dozen of us worked in the shop until the PVC strip fit like a steel band on the boat. My stubborn adherence to quality cost me a month on that one item.

I scrutinized the literature, studied the completed Balaton 31 boats, and examined *St. Jupat*. In the meantime my financial position worsened. I thank my family, friends, and acquaintances that it didn't result in any deterioration of the boat's quality. Our mobilizable valuables turned into resins, mahogany, glass-mat, stainless steel sheets, and tubes. We lived on a hill a mile and a half from the nearest bus stop, and the most difficult loss was selling our car. Stopping the purchasing and administration would have

---

[31] The gunwale (pronounced "gunnel") is the highest edge of the side of a boat, or what I would describe as the hull-deck junction.

Above: *The bow is made to be impact-resistant—The extra built-in beams/stringers in the ceiling are visible here, as is the bow furniture that has been installed to provide a stronger framework for the hull.*

stopped the boat building as well if I had not been helped.

In my life I have been well blessed, considering the number of parents I have had. My true parents supplied the genes, while the non-biological ones supplied the education. It was my stepfather Ivan Zsigmond who gave me my first boat, the *Red Fox*. He taught me not only how to put on my tie, but also how to see the world from its flipside. He came to my aid now, loaning his car to me for six months. After that I had the car of my friend Andris Lovas, and then that of my friend Szines. During this time spent running after *Salammbo*'s business, I covered a total distance equivalent to that of the Equator.

One example of the difficulties we encountered in the feverish madness of building our boat was in obtaining our mast. Because of our financial situation, only manufacturers within the country could be considered. The largest profile produced by Kofem would have been adequate, but the factory did not take individual orders. And the completed, rigged, and equipped masts that were available were of unacceptable quality and price.

We started surveying the field, visiting the factories and our friends. After a month of running around, phoning, and telexing, the mast was finally ready. Everything was satisfactory, except for the welding. I received it and promptly resold it. I started to look again for a competent welder. I found him in a shipyard in Vac. So the work started again in the Kofem factory, and two half profiles were delivered in a month. At the agreed time I hurried there with a borrowed car and trailer, but I was disappointed again. The alloy and the hardness were not as specified, so I would not accept it.

In the next month the die broke. Without any other orders coming in, its replacement wasn't considered very urgent, except by me. I fought on two fronts. I tried to find enough orders for the same product, and in the factory I urged the continuation of the work. After two months the profiles of the mast were ready (two halves of the mast had to be welded together). I could drive to Vac with the 12-meter-long profiles. But at Vac the only skilled welder was sick. So I started sickbed visits!

The problem of the surface treatment also became complicated. After driving many miles, and making numerous phone calls, I found that the country is really small. It was only possible to anodize up to six and a half meters (21 feet). No sweat... I hurried from Vac to Vecses, where, at the recommendation of a district physician friend, a small workshop agreed to tackle the double length. That was enough. I have to agree with Jozsef Gal and Nandor Fa. Before the voyage of *St. Jupat*, they said that they were already past the halfway mark of their circumnavigation as soon as they finished building their boat.

But at last the boat was finished. On the orange sides we painted, in black letters, the name of Hannibal's daughter, the princess "Salammbo."

EXCERPTS FROM THE LOG
September 3, 1990
Position: 10°33'S and 024°22'W. Heading: 190°. Speed: 5 knots. Temperature: 22-26° C (72-79° F).
At home the autumn was coming. Where I was in the southern hemisphere, spring began with alternating sunny and cloudy periods. In the evening it was overcast, but no rain came. The sea was stormy, with Force 6-7 winds. The boat heeled to 30-35°. From time to time a flying fish jumped up, but I saw no other living beings.

In the evening radio period, the topic of my discussion with Zsolt was once again my sickness. My first aid kit had been assembled by Dr. Norbert

Hudomel and his pharmacist wife, but they were difficult to reach. The way I understand it from Zsolt, they had moved from Ajka to Sopron. I needed medical advice, and Zsolt phoned all over until my radio questions were answered by one of the experts at the pharmacology center in Fejer County. I had to treat my stomach pains with Massigel-K. I rummaged in the boxes until I found it. What I wouldn't have given to get rid of the pain and depression I was suffering…

September 5, 1990

I wrote in all capital letters: "THE FIRST DAY I CAN ENJOY OCEAN SAILING FULLY." I had truly been waiting two long months for it, but at last I had it. I could finally sail with my working sails. The wind was Force 4 and the sea was calmer. The deck dried, and it was a rare pleasure that the moving parts could be oiled or siliconed peacefully.

I spent the rest of the day working on bottles. The ordinance people had bottled a large quantity of soda water for me. The thick-walled 1.5-liter bottles blew up one after the other, probably due to temperature and pressure changes. I poured the water into the now empty stainless steel tank, and since the carbon dioxide was gone, I put Micropur water purifying tablets into it. That way I could save about 70 liters of soda water. There was still something to be happy about. I put the leftover plastic bottles into the chain locker. This helped in four ways: they raised the buoyancy of the open locker, they could attenuate the force of a collision, I could save rainwater in them, and I didn't have to pollute the ocean by throwing them overboard. I was proud of myself for figuring it all out.

I was a maniac in how much I cared about protecting the environment. I would have liked to lighten the boat, but the only things I would ever throw into the water were food and cans, the latter of which would corrode away when they reached the bottom at 13,000 feet. I put all plastics into a bag, along with the used oils and filters. I was convinced that if I protected the ocean, it would protect me too.

September 6, 1990

The weather was pleasant and the waves abated, but I still covered 95 miles. Big shark-like fish swam around the boat. Their bodies were blue and their tails greenish-yellow. I was standing in the stern when a whale crossed *Salammbo*'s path 20 feet ahead. This led to the usual rushing around—get out the video camera bag, tear off the waterproof cover, plug in the extension cord—and of course by the time everything was together I could only see the whale's splash in the water as it disappeared again beneath the surface.

I had no luck with the video camera. I couldn't change the set's batteries. I could only operate the camera from the boat's batteries, using a

30-foot extension cord. This limited my mobility and prevented the use of the very expensive waterproof housing. I had to accept the fact that Captain Cousteau would not have a new competitor.

September 8, 1990

I passed 18° South and 021° West. I moved farther away from Brazil and closer to Africa. In doing so I deviated from my previously laid plans. It was possible that the distance would be shorter that way, or it might be longer if I ran out of wind. The wind turned unexpectedly to northwest. Its direction was good, but its strength varied all the time. I changed sails all day long.

September 9, 1990

I was hit by depression like a boat by a storm. I became lethargic. I helped my state by deciding that I would not work that day. After all, it was Sunday. Lying in my bunk, I tried to read something. After a few lines, I put the book down, went on deck, and watched the ever moving ocean. I looked at it, but I didn't want to see it. I felt that the solitude and tiredness were crushing me. I hung onto a shroud and screamed and cried.

In the afternoon, I cleaned up my act, literally, since I didn't mind using 2 liters of water for my bath. The washing and subsequent exercises shook me out of my funk.

September 10, 1990

The wind turned during the night. I slept only 50 minutes, but during that time the boat turned around and sailed north-northeast. The wind changed around all morning, until finally it settled into the seasonal southeast. Its intensity did not stick to the predictions, but it gradually strengthened, and in the evening it became a veritable storm.

At 1900 hours, I threw up my lunch and snacks at the same time. I made up for the loss with a sumptuous dinner. It was not in vain, because a little later I needed all my energy. Around 2200 hours, a 60-knot wind stressed the rigging and my nerves. The stormy sea continuously lifted *Salammbo* on huge waves, only to drop her again. I had taken off the vent cowls (coamings) to make the insides airtight. Air did not come into the cabin, but a lot of seawater did. It leaked everywhere, through the vents as well as through portholes and the hatch. Somehow the radio got wet too.

The night was torture, and this was still only the Atlantic Ocean. What would happen when I reached the wild waters of the Indian Ocean and the Roaring Forties, towards which I was fighting with the determination of a masochist?

September 12, 1990

At dawn I made a vow that I would not let another night like this happen to me. Poor *Salammbo* was nearly torn apart. I should have changed down the sails earlier. I set the 6-square-meter (65-square-foot) storm jib and furled the main. I still covered over 100 n. miles in the hard-blowing wind. Short of the Tropic of Capricorn I had to put on my boots and woolen watch cap. On top of it all I felt ill again. My urine was murky and I felt a strong stab in my side. I knew that I did not have appendicitis, but even to think of it gave me a cold sweat. I should diet, but if I didn't eat I would lose my energy reserves. The initially beneficial Massigel tablets were not helping anymore.

September 14, 1990

At 1:00 in the morning, I crossed the Tropic of Capricorn. If I could, I would have celebrated even more, for it was Zsuzsa's birthday. Thinking of my family and home, I just wanted to get back and never again go on the oceans.

Increasingly I caught myself swearing. I was worn by the wave motion—not so much physically as in my nerves. I didn't have enough grabbing extremities. For the first time I thought of apes with envy. When I was cooking, pots flew in a hundred directions, and the dinner often landed on the cabin ceiling. I used one of my hands to hang on, while one leg and my bottom tightened me to the bulkhead. The other leg pushed the water pump, and the remaining hand did the cooking. I often spilled hot water when I was warming food on the gimbaled gas-burner; my right forearm was covered in burn marks.

Experts call the Trade Winds a piece of cake. I always thought I had a sweet tooth, but it really must have been extraordinary weather. The reason was probably the maximum amount of sunspot activity. One thing was certain—the Doldrums that usually stopped sailors for a week had apparently retired. *Salammbo* galloped through like a hard-driven horse.

September 15, 1990

It was Saturday, and as I understood from the radio, the BOC fleet was starting from Newport. The organizers were real old salts; they wouldn't start the race on a Friday. If everything went well, Nandi Fa would soon report on the airwaves. To make it easy he would use the call name "VIZES" (Hungarian for "wet"). Our other friend named Nandi, who was the most active member of the Hungarian circle in Sao Paolo, would come in as "SZÁRAZ" (Hungarian for "dry"). We were waiting with great anticipation for news about "wet" Nandi. The weather was improving, so I washed up and exercised. I felt much better.

September 16, 1990

Looking at the calendar, I could hardly believe it. I had started from Pola exactly 3 months before. It felt like 10 years. In the morning an ivory gull and a frigate bird ate 3 cans of blade stew, 2 turkey pâtés, and a peachy-flavored fish. The last was taken down least willingly. It seemed that their taste was similar to mine.

September 18, 1990

Hurrah! The weather was excellent, with Force 4 northeast winds and moderate waves. My activities centered around the motor. I changed the oil and the filter, cleaned the water strainer, tightened the V belt, and generally lubricated.

At the wheel in the afternoon, I couldn't believe my eyes. A huge steel tank was floating not very far from the boat. It was at least as large as *Salammbo*. I was frightened, because there was no way I could have spotted it during the night. Maybe with a good radar, but I had none. However, I had the Great Caretaker with me, who guided me well in my seafaring.

The 1- to 2-hour daily sleeping times did not allow much rest. From then on, I had to scan the horizon longer and more alertly with my binoculars.

September 20, 1990

The wind abated; the sea did not. *Salammbo* rolled a lot. The most intensely moving part was the stern. It reminded me of the focs'l[32] of the M/V *Borsod*, where I was billeted as a deck boy. To this day I can feel the fetid, stagnant air, which was a result of a lack of ventilation in the forepeak. I can still hear the ear-splitting rumbling of the anchor chain, and I can see myself wedged into the elevated bunk to avoid being tossed out of it by the heaving.

On *Salammbo* I could not sleep in the V-berth, because it was used for storage. Under the cushions were food and tools. In the front cupboard was the medicine chest, and on the berths I kept eleven more sails. The crammed-in stores reached to the top, but the crazy motion and strong blows always caused something to fly out. I started my preparations for the worst storms of the Roaring Forties by fixing the stuff with fishing net. I also covered the sharp corners of the nav. station and the table with polyfoam, and I put anti-skid strips on the floor.

The air was getting cooler and the thermometer showed 18° C (64° F), but in the sprinkling rain and Force 5 northwest wind I was definitely cold.

---

[32] The focs'l (aka "fo'c'sle" or "forecastle") of a ship is the section of the bow below the deck, which would often be the location of the crew's living quarters.

My position was 30°25'S and 024°22'W. I reckoned that it would take a week to reach the 40° Latitude. I dictated a mad tempo. I changed the running rigging, and adjusted the blades of the wind generator and its stand. I hoped that they would withstand the 80- to 90-knot winds. In my great hurry I was clumsy. While refilling the Stelton lamp with kerosene, I cracked its glass. I was afraid that it would not last long, and it was my only heater.

In the evening I developed new yoga exercises to try to bathe myself in the sink. The permitted amount of water could not exceed one and a half to two liters. Apart from the bath, my spirits were lifted when I received the broadcasts of "My Homeland" and Radio Free Europe.[33]

September 21, 1990

The sun was shining, but the cirrus clouds thickened and the barometer steadily sank. The northwest wind increased and reached Force 8. As soon as I set a jib I had to go and change it to a smaller one. I closed the air vent of the storage area and the shutoff valve of the engine exhaust. I stored the floorboards of the cockpit in the cabin and removed the filters from the cockpit drain holes. Everything had to be tied down securely.

Zsuzsa and Andris Lovas were at the Equator radio station when I established contact. I pushed my feet to the bulkheads of the boat so I would not fall away from the set. It would be nice to know more about the family, but we could only exchange a few hurried words. The huge waves buried the boat, and water squirted through the closed boards of the companionway hatch. I swore at the sea for not permitting me to hear my wife's voice.

September 22, 1990

The waves accelerated me to frightening speeds. I had never sailed in such wind and waves before. I slammed from one side to another in the cabin, and praised my brains that I had padded the furniture. My 38-foot-tall mast, which seemed like a smokestack on Lake Balaton, was now bending like a reed. Now I knew it was impossible for anything on the sea to be oversized.

So far my bed had been a foam mattress on the cabin floor between the bunks. It seemed to be the best place, since I could not fly sideways. But since it was the lowest point in the cabin, it was also the coldest. Counting on falling temperatures and an eventual capsize, I decided to change sleeping places. I emptied the pilot berth behind the chart table, which

---

[33] "My Homeland" (a more direct translation would be "birthplace") was a radio station transmitted overseas for Hungarians outside of the country. Radio Free Europe is an international radio broadcast historically rooted in efforts to freely spread news in opposition to communism and the censorship and propaganda that went along with it.

could only be approached from the companionway. My claustrophobia in that tiny space was mitigated by a small porthole that allowed me a look at the steering wheel. The space was so small that I could warm it with my breath. And I needed to, even though I had already pulled on my long johns and thermal shirts.

The albatrosses visited me more often. They didn't like to land on the madly swirling waters. The young ones darted between the waves, showing off and wasting their energy. The older ones glided with masterly technique and aristocratic bearing through the lees of wave cliffs. The sight of them inspired quieting timelessness. I wanted to fly with them, far away from here.

FREEZING TROPICS

The last days of September did not fly; they crawled. The weather changed in monotonous sequences of tolerably moderate and stormy winds. The southerly gales brought cold winds, and to my great annoyance, pushed me north. It was difficult to get away from the 34° South Latitude, although I had planned to reach the 0° Longitude—which was only 7° away—at 40° South.

On September 24, I was 300 miles to the southwest of the island group of Tristan da Cunha. These islands were more than a thousand miles from Cape Town in South Africa.

The nearness of the African continent manifested itself when I received Morse code weather reports from the coastal stations at Cape Town. The operators worked fast and accurately. Their storm and gale warnings were reliable, but I had to add 24 hours. The gale predicted for the 26th arrived with the Force 8 winds a day later.

I received good news from the Equator station about Nandi Fa, who was sailing toward Cape Town after the start of the race in Newport. His longitude of 032°32' was identical to mine, but the field of BOC racers was still in the Northern Hemisphere.

I felt the cold more now, mainly because of the humidity. I wore my cap even in the cabin. I wrapped toilet paper between the two socks in my boots. I held my warm clothes in the highest regard, and it sometimes prompted me to achieve impossible feats. My woolen watch cap from Hamburg fell into the water during a sail change. I turned back despite the wind, and with careful maneuvering, I hooked it out of the water. The 8-10° C (46-50° F) temperature at the helm forced me to change the fashion of my outfit. Over the long "undies" I donned "Maca," an overall lined with fake fur. Over this layer came my moldy pullover[34] and the foul weather

---

[34] With the constant dampness and humidity, it was difficult to avoid the unpleasant reality of having a moldy pullover.

gear. Much of my outfit had been a gift from the military. I had fur-lined general's high boots on my feet. I could have scored high in a Halloween costume contest.

I entered the tenth month in this fashionable outfit.

5

IN THE ROARING FORTIES
(1990 September 29 — October 24)

"Oh God, be good to me; the sea is so wide, and my ship is so small."

—Breton Fisherman's Prayer

T HE WEATHER DIDN'T SHOW ANY GREAT VARIETY IN THE last days of September. The dampness was more and more aggravating. Condensation covered the ceiling of the cabin.[35] The temperature in the cabin was 10-12° C (50-54° F), while outside it was 8-9° C (46-48° F), but the wind chill factor made it feel much colder.

The only way to maintain my energy was to eat more frequently. I tried to make meals more colorful. When you are out at sea, eating actually serves multiple functions. Beyond the biological necessity, it also provides an opportunity for a social event, and it is sometimes the sole source of physical pleasure. I don't have to mention that for single-handers, the only meal companions to be found are limited to weevils in flour, rice, etc., but the point about enjoyment cannot be neglected.

I have never been a gourmet, but now I felt a strong drive to break out of the monotony. My first attempts were feeble. For example, I mixed onions, garlic, mustard, and chili in various proportions and added the

---

[35] Contrary to most commercially sold yachts, *Salammbo* did not have a liner on the inside of the deck, which would have provided cosmetic coverage and prevented the buildup of condensation on the ceiling of the cabin. This was a deliberate design choice, as it allowed access to parts on the underside of the deck, allowing for repairs or adjustments much more easily.

mixture to ground ham to create a pâté. Next, more boldly, I made meatballs with tomato from "de-cabbaged" stuffed cabbage and ketchup. Then I washed the sourness from Vecsés cabbage, roasted it in caramel, and added pasta to it to make a cabbage "Cvekedli" a la Salammbo. On the other hand, I started to neglect bread baking. It took too much time and propane. The frequent gales also helped to discontinue this complicated and tiresome procedure.

On both September 26 and 27 I completed the 150 n. mile norm, which lifted my spirits in spite of the biting cold. The next day a gale arrived that had been predicted for a day earlier. Two squids were also thrown aboard by the waves. These were prepared by frying in garlic oil. As I ate them, I had to admit to myself with some chagrin that I had lowered my standards. Holidays were marked by events such as changing my underwear, or a possible wash-up. I was forced more often to use the hygiene of the court of Louis XIV: cleaning myself with cotton wool and baby powder.

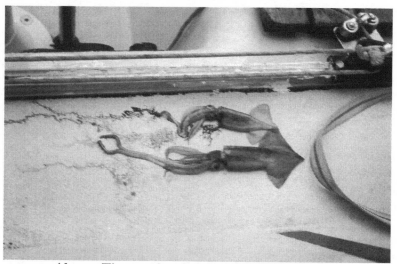

Above: *These squid washed up on deck for another meal. Everything tastes good when you are on a canned-food diet!*

Over the next two days the wind was either from the southeast or from the southwest, and seldom below gale force. The temperature rarely went above 9° C (48° F), and the humidity was 65-70%. On September 29 there was good news and bad news—I crossed the Greenwich Meridian to get to the eastern longitudes, but I had drunk the last of my wine. I had plenty of water though, since it rained for two days straight. I couldn't catch it, unfortunately, because the waves reached as high as the sails and made the water too salty. The wind turned around and I went back to the Western Hemisphere again. I increased my latitude, which was chilling, literally, since

I was cold more often as a result. I acquired more living space by consuming my stores, and *Salammbo*'s motion became freer as a result. I moved around more and more like a bear, for every day I had to add another layer to my clothes.

I was down at the dreaded 40° South Latitude. My course for the next 2 months would be to the east. I tried not to think about it. To avoid depression, I chose the tactic of daily survival. Every survived day was like reaching one more safe hold on a steep rock face.

AT THE MEETING OF OCEANS

I tried to solve the riddle of the birds: why were so many of them attracted to this barren, forbidding region? Was it because the water was richer in plankton and fish, or was it just to be away from humanity and pollution? Maybe to find complete freedom for themselves in those latitudes, or more likely all of these factors combined. Legends say that the albatross flies around the world for seven years, and then builds its nest to raise its only chick. I admit that at first I did not care much for birds, although I generally like animals, but the birds of the Southern Ocean amazed me with their extraordinary toughness. For me, the albatross became the symbol of freedom.

Above: *The albatrosses were my most loyal companions in the Southern Ocean.*

My breath could be seen in the cabin most of the time. The humidity was seldom below 75%. My weekends were not tied to the calendar, but nature, it seemed, kept itself to the ritual. With some regularity it permitted me a bit of rest every 7-10 days. These rest days were relatively quiet, with the wind reduced to Force 6-7 from its regular frenzy. What would normally be considered a gale force wind seemed like a calm lull in that place. As a defense against the depressing environs, I changed my readings to the light comical foreign legion stories of Rejto.[36] The sparkling humor substituted for the sun and separated me from the constant heaving and crashing world around me.

The radio periods in the evening took an interesting turn. Nandi performed on the air, and what really surprised me were his fans. They had no radio permit, yet spoke directly to him. I switched the set off in a hurry. The silence of the hams of the Equator Club showed that they agreed with me.[37]

On the 7th of October the boat was jumping around so wildly that I had to tie myself down in the cabin. A Force 10 northwesterly was screaming in the rigging. The waves had grown to giant-sized and they battered *Salammbo* with ceaseless energy. My attempt to cook ended with everything on the floor, including myself. There was not a dry spot, nor a salt-free garment. As if the 80% humidity were not enough, the rain often generously chipped in to make the conditions more unpleasant. The propane igniter had enough and gave up.

The next day at noon, a 50-foot whale inspected me. At the first meeting it came across about 150 feet away, then turned around and passed me twice. As it approached closer every time, I tolled the boat's bell and blew the horn as much as I could. The acoustic defense was successful, and the whale left indignantly.

I was never afraid of these huge mammals. I always felt electrified on the numerous occasions when we met. The existence and essence of body language is best expressed by the mammals of the sea. The energetic dolphins frolicking around the boat showed with every move their togetherness, their renewing contacts, and their harmony. As the albatrosses signify freedom for me, the dolphins represent happy optimism. Whales radiate benevolence with their majestic swimming style, which typifies those magnificent creatures.

My lack of fear didn't mean that I wasn't aware of the danger. Many yachts have been sunk by collisions with whales, and these incidents were becoming more frequent. There are more whales around, because of the

---

[36] Jeno Rejto (Refer to Footnote 21, pg. 46.)

[37] By this point Nandi had become a well-known figure in Hungary due to the promotional campaigns related to his sailing adventures. Hence he had the ability to draw a crowd, which unfortunately also included unlicensed ham radio operators. Hams have strict rules of communication (i.e. no vulgarity, no politicizing, etc.). These fans of Nandi were breaking the rules and causing problems, and we wanted to distance ourselves from their inappropriate behavior.

effective protection measures, as well as more offshore yachts. A sleeping whale's reflex to a collision causes serious and sometimes even fatal damage to a boat. Also, the underbody of modern sailboats looks very similar to some sea mammals when viewed from below. The sight of most sea creatures is weak, and the investigation of a romantic possibility may occur. This was in my thoughts when I tolled the bell to show that *Salammbo* was spoken for.

The combination of single-handing and permanently rough seas doesn't favor videotaping. I put the camera into a waterproof bag and stowed it where it could resist the wildest motion. The interesting scenes were seldom long-lasting, and when I dug out and set up the camera the show was usually over already. In this case my luck was out, because the tape finished in my camera. As a consolation I crossed Cape Town's meridian. I would soon be in the Indian Ocean.

Just before midnight on the 10th of October, I crossed the 020° East meridian, which is the border between the Atlantic and Indian Oceans. It was the third time that it had happened to me, but this time it was quite different than before. During the Egypt-Israel war Hungarian ships rounded Africa to get to India or the Far East. We used to moor in Durban to take on fuel. This time I only went there in my thoughts, though the temptation to follow through on the stop was strong.

The weather savagely pulled me back into action. A storm turning from west to south blew at Force 10-11. Huge seas built upon 20-foot swells. The boat rattled under constant blows, and the water streamed through the closed boards. I tried to celebrate despite the raging war around me. The canned wieners were prepared without much ado, and at midnight the military chicken needed only a quick warm-up.

I rounded the first of the five Southern Capes, and I have to admit that I was very apprehensive about it. The Cape of Good Hope, contrary to its name, is a stormy and dangerous area. For mariners, the neighboring Cape Agulhas is the milestone. The Agulhas current comes between Africa and Madagascar and meets the southwest storms head-on at this point. This produces difficult, treacherous conditions. Its bad reputation comes from the Agulhas Bank, which is a 600-foot-deep continuation of the African continental shelf. In the shallower sea the waves are steep and nearly square-shaped. This cemetery of ships still regularly acquires new members. To reduce the risk I went farther south, avoiding the Bank by a large margin. I entered the Indian Ocean at 40° Latitude, hundreds of miles south of the African continent.

I had covered over 10,000 miles so far, about one third of the voyage. Ahead of me lay 4,800 miles to Australia—a section with a very bad reputation that I had to cover within 50 days. I had been underway for four months, and I had not seen a human being for nearly two and a half months. Interestingly this disturbed me the least—or to be more precise, it was really only the absence of certain people that actually hurt me. Rather than dwelling on my isolation from the rest of the human race, I spent more time dreaming about a hot shower and a dry, warm, and steady bed where I could have 3 to 4 hours of undisturbed sleep. Nature accepted that wish, and on the 12th I was given a whole day to relax. I discovered that I was not the only one getting worn out. There was galvanic corrosion between the aluminum mast and the stainless steel fittings, despite the interlay and sacrificial metal. It was not the only place where I had problems with electricity; the Sat. Nav. also gave up.

Apart from the radio, which basically provides psychological assistance, the satellite navigator was my last working piece of equipment linking my navigation to the twentieth century. Now I was reminded just how much I had become complacent—and in a way, lazy—about my methods of navigation. It was the end of taking it easy and having hour-long sleeps. Now I had to always be prepared for a celestial sight. It would not have been such a great headache on quieter, sunny seas. But here, where for days I could not see a blue patch in the sky, much less a celestial body, it made me very nervous. The constant overcast sky, and the boat dancing on the huge waves like a cork, permitted only sighting the sun and moon, and only under extreme conditions. The Good Lord had enough of my bellyaching and sent me a new Force 10 northeast storm. *Salammbo* ran at 8 knots under a 50-squarefoot storm jib. Raindrops hit me in the face like bullets.

On the 15th of October I flew at 10-12 knots with the 50-squarefoot sail, far above the theoretical hull speed of the boat. On the more favorable starboard tack, the galley swam on the port side. This worked in my favor, because the pooling water would drain out through the sink as the boat heeled to port. The port tack was far worse, as the chart table and my bunk were left underwater. This determined how colorful my vocabulary was, as I chose tacks responding to the wind changes.

EXCERPTS FROM THE LOG
October 16, 1990
Position: 40°40'S and 031°06'E. Wind: Force 10-12 W. Temperature: 10° C (50° F). Humidity: 80%. Rain fronts, showers.
This data doesn't say much. It may not mean much if I add that the wind speed and sea state were peak values. I didn't dare to leave the wheel from 3:00 in the morning to 5:00 in the evening. I couldn't leave *Salammbo* to the wind vane steering. A new high sea built on the 20- to 25-foot swells, and the wave height was 45-50 feet. I did what I could, and then I prayed.

But I left praying for last... First I went over everything I had learned and experienced in my life. I sheeted the storm jib to the center, but I could lower the storm trysail only at about 4:00 in the afternoon, when the storm abated to Force 10-11. If I had tried it earlier, it would have been torn to pieces. The 75-knot wind nearly choked me. Its sound was quite unbearable out on the deck. During my turbulent life I had survived a lot, but never such raging forces. The idea of infinity starts to take a plausible, measurable shape. I could not fathom how the storm could keep increasing. It must have an upper limit...

Then I realized my mistake. I had immersed myself so much with the details of storm sailing that, in the excitement of surfing between the rogues, I had sailed directly towards the storm's center. After a 180° turn, I put out the Bruce anchor to serve as a drogue and reduce *Salammbo*'s broaching. To my surprise, the 26-pound anchor on the end of a 150-foot rode danced on the water like a ping pong ball. With a 300-foot line it started to work, only jumping to the surface at some of the wildest surf rides.

I was very tired and the fear also reduced my reserves. In my "waterproof" weather gear, the only dry item was a NATO slice wrapped in foil. I tried to eat it with numb fingers. I thought wistfully of my leather boots, which I had left in the cabin because they had slippery soles. My legs were numb from the cold and the stiff stance I was forced to maintain. The only item that gave me satisfaction was my pilot cap that I had inherited from my grandfather. My grandmother had embroidered his initials into its leather lining. After I buttoned the ear flaps under my chin, a feeling of warmth went through me, and the raging wind lost a few decibels. My muscles steered the boat in a subconscious routine and I didn't see the towering waves anymore...

* * *

I crouch like a stowaway on my grandfather's biplane. We glide, with the motor stopped, between the low-lying, dense clouds. The cap is not on me but on my grandfather, with his goggles, though they may not help him much in the swirling white mass. The dipping plane tears out of the cloud cover, and the silvery bends of the Isonzo River nearly blind me. The emplacements become visible, and the machine gunner shatters his camera. An approaching Italian fighter plane ends the reconnaissance. Grandfather turns sharply with a howling motor.[38]

Jumping over the dicey situation, I ride on his knees beside the pleasant murmurs of the tiled stove, playing with the buckle of his belt. Dudu—I gave him this name because of his scolding[39]—mixes some pleasantly

---

[38] My grandfather served as a spy for Austria-Hungary during World War I.

[39] While my grandfather was a perfectly regimented war veteran, I was a nonstop troublemaker at a young age. Hence I was well accustomed to his scolding "du-du" (akin to "tsk-tsk") and found it only

scented Club tobacco into his smelly 'garden tobacco,' because of my Grandmother, and fills his pipe. He sinks contentedly into the carved, velvety armchair, and I into his lap. Then we decipher the calligraphy of heavy codices; at other times we go over Zichy or Durer drawings. Quickly changing scenes, we sculpt the most lifelike snowman on the street. The time flies as the veteran pilot and I are in a summer garden. Starting the day early, we hurry toward the neatly aligned vegetable beds. The string pulled taut between the bayonets[40] directs us, and we happily gather the mole cricket grubs out of the sunken pots used as traps. As a reward we nip unwashed grapes from the arbor.

As my hunting grounds extend, his shrink. His resilient vitality impresses me in spite of his failing health. With his remote guidance I carry his hidden relics down from the attic, and the yellowing faded newspaper pins me beside him again. We evaluate the events of '56,[41] taking time with the details... Hearing my coded doorbell ring he only goes to the window. I still see his head, with the hairnet, watching me with bright eyes through the curtain as I jump over the high fence. Despite his suffering hands, he is still looking for the answers as a talented self-taught man. His example engraved in me, better than Hemingway's pen, the invincibility of men.

Those were my thoughts when saying goodbye to my mother and to him before departing on my voyage. I had arrived at the cemetery too late, finding the gates closed before me as usual. Climbing over the cemetery wall in the dark, I felt his warm encouraging gaze that always gave me strength when encountering obstacles.

* * *

The bitter art of hand steering tied me to the helm for endless hours. I didn't dare to go down into the cabin during the night. Even though there wasn't much chance of meeting another ship, I preferred to time my short rests for daylight hours, when I trusted that *Salammbo* was more easily visible.

The unremitting presence of danger choreographed my movements in the cabin as much as on deck. I numbly tore down my oilies and contorted

---

natural to give him as a nickname.

[40] The actual World War I-era bayonets that my grandfather used as stakes in his garden were the perfect representation of his innovation, organization, and high standards in everything he did—much of which came from his war experience.

[41] "We evaluate the events of '56": referring to the Hungarian revolution against the communist government and the invading Soviets in 1956.

myself into the sleeping bag of my coffin-bunk. I stuffed in the two woolen blankets to defend against the cold that penetrated my bones. The water streaming in through the washboards didn't bypass my bedcovers, and I felt the moisture through my clothes. I knew that if I were ever to relate my experiences, I would emphasize the importance of using natural materials! Wool kept my body warm despite the moisture, and I didn't experience any fungi on my skin.

To maintain my energy level I tried to keep to the 30-minute rest periods during the day. Sleep would descend on me suddenly in the slowly drying sleeping bag. It left only a few seconds to genuflect and say a brief prayer. I slept, but I knew that my internal clock would pull me back into the state of wakeful readiness after exactly 30 minutes.

Above: *My home (or jail) for a year: the inside of the cabin, with my "coffin bunk" visible on the left.*

THE TECHNIQUES OF SURVIVAL

For days I felt that the wildly rolling boat, the damp, the cold, my concern about my family, the loneliness, and the pangs of fear were the adversaries against my willpower. If I lost the battle and could not meet the strain physically or mentally, I would lose my control over the boat. The date jotted down in the log, October 17, reminded me that I had been underway for four months. I tried to think of the past: what had I survived so far, what had I succeeded in through my prodigious efforts? With this I tried to maintain my mental equilibrium, rather than thinking about what lay ahead.

In the region of the Roaring Forties my whole outlook was transformed. It shrunk to periods of days or hours, sometimes only minutes, during which I had to survive and cover more and more miles. The old overused

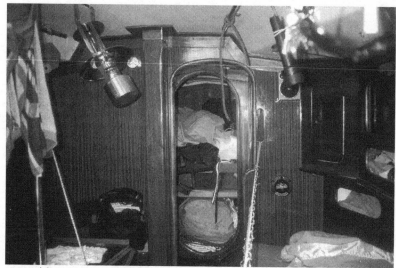

Above: *A view of the forward cabin, completely packed with sails.*

legion slogan "march or die" consumed my mind. I was dragged like a man possessed by life's instincts towards the east. It haunted me that my slow progress would worsen my chances of passing Cape Horn, and that spurred me to increase my pace on the Indian Ocean.

My most forbidding dreams seemed to materialize in those days. The South Indian Ocean is not the devil of single-handers by accident. The Southern Ocean in the region of 40-50° Latitude is mostly stormy, depending on the seasons. The westerlies follow the general direction of the passing cyclones, but it is not necessarily identical to the actual wind direction. The winds there, which often blow at speeds over 60 knots, can freely generate waves that will not be diminished by any continent or other land mass. The waves can grow unhindered, which makes this area unique among the world's oceans. Navigation in the Southern Oceans is made more difficult by bad visibility, significant amounts of rain, snow, hail, low temperatures, high humidity, and the chance of collision—rarely with an island, but more often with icebergs or whales. The Indian Ocean heaps on top of these factors its own unpredictability, with frequently changing wind patterns and the mixed unruly waves that are caused by them.

Since it was impossible to stop and disembark, I tried to shape and perfect my storm sailing and survival methods. In my daily radio reports I mostly just reported that I was "in the orange," referring to my orange-colored storm sails. The purpose of the 50-square-foot storm jib and 60-square-foot storm trysail was not only to power the boat, but to make it maneuverable as well. The running or broad reaching *Salammbo* often heeled

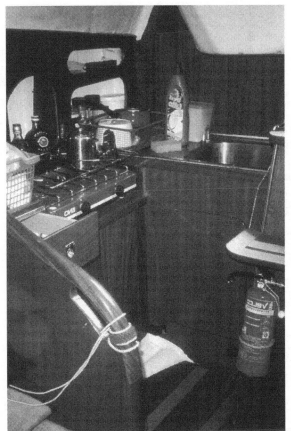

Above: *A view of the galley, seen here in a rare vertical position, contrary to what I was used to.*

and submerged her overly curved sides into the water. This disrupted her symmetrical floating position and pushed her windward, like a bobsled is turned by a sharp bend. *Salammbo* would lose her speed and consequent maneuverability during this broaching. So when I was on a broad reach or running, I didn't use the jib in the usual way, but instead sheeted it to the centerline. This diminished *Salammbo*'s broaching tendencies. In following seas, sheeting the jib to the centerline allowed it to act as a vertical plane foil. If a following and overtaking sea were to push the exposed stern of a boat to the side, it would become fully exposed to the wind and, moving sideways, it would become impossible to steer. But the jib sheeted in the middle could prevent this by turning the boat back to its course.

Salammbo often turned away from the wind, jibing the trysail. Since the trysail was not rigged to the boom, a jibe only rolled the boat. It did not

Above: *Sailing in the Roaring Forties: here the centered storm jib keeps the bow downwind and works as a broach preventer. The point of sail is broad reach. In this photo, even the trysail is dropped due to the heavy weather.*

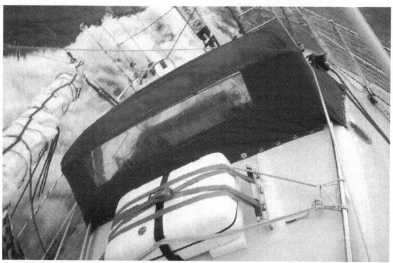

Above: *Sailing in the Roaring Forties, with the same sail arrangement as the previous photo, but looking towards the aft section of the boat during the storm ride. My life raft is also visible in this photo.*

cause any harm, as it would have with the traditional reefed mainsail. In the hardest storms, even the 60-square-foot trysail proved to be too much, and under bare poles the boat still charged like a speedboat. When that was the case, the best way to maintain control on my boat was to pull a drogue. This was the purpose of the Bruce anchor towed by a 250- to 300-foot rope. As previously mentioned, it would reduce the boat's speed and make it steerable. In the critical Force 11-12 winds, I did not let the boat sail directly downwind. I had to change my heading to sail on broad reaches instead, with occasional jibes.[42]   As I sailed away from the African continent, I stowed my detailed charts and instead used the monthly Pilot Charts, even for navigation. These charts cannot be used for coastal navigation requiring great accuracy, but they give the basic information about the weather and sea conditions to be expected, including the wind speed and direction, ice conditions, humidity, barometric pressure, and probability of storms. It was my habit to mark on the chart not only the daily position of *Salammbo*, but also the direction of lows and fronts as I received them from the coastal stations. The line showing *Salammbo*'s progress was a number of zigzags. I would have liked to run directly without detours on the 40° parallel, but my sense of caution in this stormy area overcame my impatience.

On the raging waters I drilled responsibility into myself as a mental exercise. I could only succeed when in my mind I tied the success of my endeavor with the fate and future of my family. As much as possible on the Southern Ocean, I tried to minimize the risks and take the longer route when necessary to sail around the storm centers. Even in my worst condition I tried to weigh every move and calculate the consequences. I needed to overpower my own nature. As a person of quick temperament and responses, I had to force myself to slow down and hold back my immediate reactions. Among the many new insights I gained was that in nature there is no place for hurry, showoffs, or the wasting of energy.

The ocean can forgive minor transgressions, but seldom major ones.

EXCERPTS FROM THE LOG
October 17, 1990
Position: 39°46'S and 032°14'E. Wind: Force 5-7. Temperature: 10° C (50° F). Humidity: 58%.
The previous storm chased me to the 41° Latitude. I tried to fight my way back. The daily 60 n. mile progress was disappointingly slow, and my mood was not helped when the fast-moving dark gray clouds in the sky showered

---

[42] Sailing 50-60° away from a directly downwind course allowed me to avoid an accidental jibe, broach, or capsize. The adjustment lengthened the distance traveled, but also made for faster sailing at the same time.

Above: *This photo was also taken while storm riding in the Roaring Forties, and it shows one of the risks of downwind sailing (in addition to broaching and the accidental jibe): being flooded in the stern by following breakers.*

me with walnut-sized hailstones.

At least the wind was steady. I could find refuge in the cabin, where the drumming of the ice outside gave a new dimension to the inexhaustible repertoire of noises. I found my way in the cacophony. The boat was thrown about by 15- to 20-foot waves. Wedged in my bunk, I felt as if I were sitting under a huge waterfall. The constant battering of the water masses was interrupted every few seconds by loud crashes when the bow of the boat slammed into the waves, or the ocean hammered the deck or the superstructure. I could distinguish between the noises even when asleep. I put Styrofoam and soft foam between the stores, stuffing it into every gap, to prevent the noise of their movements from distracting my attention. When I could, I greased and oiled every moving part, from the range to the motor, so their squeals and rattles would not increase the chaos. The creaking of the mahogany steps of the companionway made me nervous, until with great difficulty I cured it by taping the edges and gaps. All of these efforts were important to ensure that the incidental noises stemming from the motion of the boat could be differentiated from noises predicting danger. In that orgy of sounds I was not disturbed in my sleep by the incidental clamor, but the noise of a flogging line or the cracking of a block sounded in my ears like an alarm trumpet.

The sea roared and pummeled us like an unstoppable air hammer.

October 19, 1990

During the night a Force 8 gale raged, and then the wind increased to Force 9. At 4:00 in the morning, the wind moderated to 30-40 knots, but turned against my sailing direction. I used the moderate conditions to open the companionway and air out the cabin.

It was perhaps because of my stress, but in the evening radio time I only complained to the Equator station and gave them a number of requests. "My heavy weather suit purchased in Vienna is not satisfactory," I said, "because it gets wet to the elbows and my pullover below it gets so soaked with salt that it is impossible to dry it out. I will try to buy a new one in Australia, or Zsuzsa should buy elbow length rubber gloves like the ones used by car wash attendants. MAHART should send an appointment calendar to Perth that I can use as a ship's log. I will need 2-foot square nylon bags for my clothes to prevent mold." I told Zsolt to note that I would need liver pâté, soy, and chocolate, as well as some red (Spanish) onions in addition to the normal onions.

October 21, 1990

The weather improved somewhat, apparently thanks to the warm front, which was not typical at this time of year. The constant head-on wind forced me to tack. It sank my heart because I judged my progress as miserable. My satellite navigator had stopped working long ago. I tried to get some sights with my sextant, using gaps in the cloud cover. My measurements were incorrect in many instances, but I still felt that I could get my position within 5-6 miles.

The shooting and the star reductions ground my nerves. For a good position I had to measure the selected body at least ten times, and it was worse if I tried to get the longitude, not just the latitude, at the noon sight. It was exhausting standing on the highest point on the heaving deck to get a glimpse of the horizon between the towering waves. It was even worse if my heading was different from the direction of the observation. I noticed that even then I tried desperately to complete the measurements rather than turn the boat. Hunting the celestial body could take more than an hour, and it was enough to push me to sail the boat 5-6 miles in the wrong direction in order to finish getting the measurement. I knew that it was stupid to worry since it was nothing compared to the thousands of miles left to Australia, but I still lamented every lost mile. There is no harder competition than racing against time.

THE GHOST OF SALAMMBO

The only pleasant surprise on the Roaring Forties was that I maintained my physical condition. The constant grabbing, balancing, and exertions of strength, even when lying down, prevented my muscles from withering.

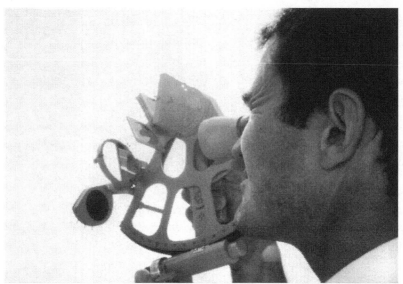

Above: *Shooting the sun with the classical instrument of navigation: the sextant. After my Sat. Nav. failed early on, the sextant was my only way to navigate for the vast majority of the circumnavigation.*

Handling the sails required hard physical work, and it was beneficial. My condition was also helped by the calisthenics I performed, gathering my willpower, even when tiredness nearly knocked me off my feet.

My thoughts and my daily routine made me realize that the greatest hazard on the 20,000-mile sail was not the storms of the ocean, but my own personality. There were no social restraints on my actions, no fans, no spectators, not even opponents to motivate me. The single-hander has to struggle against a great danger, that of fighting with his own physical and mental endurance. He could easily collapse in both body and mind. Living in the impossibly small space amid constant dangers can lead to monotony and tragic depression, unless the single-hander develops a strictly set routine and mental anchor points.

In attempting to maintain my physical and mental integrity I philosophized, read a lot, and listened to the radio. Also, what was becoming more important every day was a hearty welcome for my imaginary visitors. I had an increasing number of visitors and friends...

* * *

My memories push away the dark curtain of forgetfulness and there they come: members of my family, my teachers, friends, coworkers, dead and alive, everyone who has ever left a mark on my life, stepping one after the other on board *Salammbo*. The boat and time fly together with them. I call them often, and when they are with me I don't feel the joint-numbing cold, the clammy dampness of the sleeping bag, or the spray on my face stinging like a million needles. I don't feel the wind gusts fraying my eardrums and my nerves. I stand in the cockpit subconsciously grabbing the wheel as pictures of my life and important people from it come alive in sharp focus.

Ghosts of my loved ones show the realm of the afterlife and everlasting existence as less distant and alien. I remember the happy hours spent with my mother. I try to shout jokes and anecdotes into the wind, recalling well that the best reward for those was my mother's spirited laughter. I slide on with a grin. My brother and I are windsurfing on the Balaton in view of his shapely girlfriends. Changing the seasons, I sit in my uncle Pali's champion iceboat. The sled is overtaken only by the sound of its bronze runners on the ice. It is interesting that a cold wave crashing on my neck from behind does not detain me in wintry scenes, but rather guides my memories into the experiences of summers long past. I crouch with my grandfather on the beach of Almadi. I smile remembering the prank, when we waited in our hiding place, encouraging an "honest finder" to try to lift the wristwatch off our blanket, only for us to snatch it away with the string we had tied to it. In response to my hunger I again open my beloved mother-in-law's favorite birthday gift: a 30"-long chain of sausage. I have to watch out because Gina, my father-in-law's German Shepherd dog, is showing an unusual interest in me...

* * *

I learned from the radio that my Komondor, Macko, was now sniffing around in the other world. The news of his death was too fresh, and pulled me back to the deck from my reverie. My teeth were chattering, and not just from the cold. I would like to tell the person who poisoned him in our backyard in Almadi that he got what he wanted—he caused immense pain.[43]

I didn't have to pull the Equator hams, Zsolt and Karcsi, from my memories, for I heard them every day. Their masterful handling of their equipment and their human values pulled them across tens of thousands of miles. I felt their closeness even when the radio was silent. After only a few words we would know each other's mood. Sometimes they acted as an

---

[43] Komondors are a breed of white dogs with distinctive, mop-like coats. They were traditionally bred as dogs who could be easily recognized at night when fulfilling their role guarding herds of sheep. They would protect the herd and were ready to attack bears that tried to harm the sheep. Our Komondor's name, "Macko," was the nickname for "Little Bear," or "Teddy Bear."

emotional dustbin, gathering my outbursts about the circumstances I was facing. Sometimes they forcibly lifted my spirits. Mixing afternoons with dawns, days, and nights, they spent more time with me than with their families. After a transmission, after the goodbyes, I was still with them in my mind as they scampered down Oreghegy (Old Mountain) like Laurel and Hardy to catch the last bus.

Another necessary piece of equipment to maintain my mental balance was the cassette player in my broadcast radio. According to my mood, it could be a Chopin prelude or Wagner's Ride of the Valkyries with which I tried to suppress the screaming of the wind and the roaring of the waves. Often the raging storm was outdone only by Queen's "Who Wants to Live Forever," which made me a "highlander" too.

I fought the elements with supernatural powers. If the weather improved and the sun came out, I would enjoy the world with Louis Armstrong, and if the sun went away I tried to conjure it with Paul Simon. I stowed ladies away on the boat too, and it was difficult to decide among Sade, Dorottya Udvaros, or Kiri Te Kanawa. However, the top of the list in the cabin was András Kern; his raspy voice was almost erased because of the constant playing. The lyrics of his songs had an important role in my valuation. I also liked Zoltán Kocsis, primarily for his political convictions, but I played his piano music because it lifted me from my daily misery into another sphere.

The best conserver of my mental health was the extensive library I took with me. My favorites ranged from Churchill to Attenborough to Kenneth Clark. The extraordinary circumstances were responsible for the reading experiences I had never had before. I had never spent so much time with thoughts and ideas, and I could now identify much more profoundly with the concepts of the books. The Southern Ocean deepens perception, clarifies the thoughts to unusual sharpness, and reorganizes values.

The sea, as if wanting to make up for the fight to survive, rewards the lonely sailor's physical pain with spiritual rebirth. That is why on the Southern Ocean it is not the house-sized waves or sail-ripping winds that hit you the hardest. The real miracle is that you can find answers to the great questions of life. You can achieve a detached view and sensory fulfillment that would otherwise only be possible by staying several decades in a Lama Monastery.

EXCERPTS FROM THE LOG
October 24, 1990

The wind speed was a steady Force 8-9 with hard gusts. The boat's speed was 6 knots with reefed jib. I could not stop wondering how my canvas had survived those pressures for so long. Not one of my sails had been torn up by the winds. A wave threw a cuttlefish into the cockpit, but I had no time to spend on it, so I sent it back home into the sea.

Because of a wind change during the night, I couldn't follow my intended course, and I had to go farther south. I was surprised by the best performance of the boat to date. During the last day we covered 165 n. miles. True, the wind had started from 8 on the Beaufort Scale and went up to 12. I started to wonder how long ago it was that I had seen my last ship. I was not surprised that even high performance steamers avoided these waters.

The radio reception from the Equator Station that evening was excellent. Zsolt passed on an interesting message. The students of the Albert Vetesi High School had invited me to their school, upon my return, to give a presentation. In the meantime they studied and tracked the path of *Salammbo*.

The consideration of the students touched me, as always when I received messages showing concern for my wellbeing. A lecture about geography in a cozy warm room before a blackboard… This whole idea seemed to be quite impossible and anachronistic to me in the midst of the globe's craziest geography.

6

THE CAPSIZE
(1990 October 21 — November 18)

"There is a patience of the wild-dogged, tireless, persistent as life itself—that holds motionless for endless hours the spider in its web, the snake in its coils, the panther in its ambuscade; this patience belongs peculiarly to life when it hunts its living food..."
—Jack London, *The Call of the Wild*

No MATTER HOW I CALCULATED IT, I WAS GUARANTEED to enjoy the hospitality of the Indian Ocean for at least another month. Or to say it as I really felt, I would be trapped as the prisoner of that cruel ocean for another grueling month. I tried not to think of how many days' fights and fearful nights were between me and the shore. But any time I heard the Morse messages of the coast station in Perth, I was seized by the wish to be where these impersonal di-di-dah's were coming from.

ON RAGING WATERS

Weather information for mariners for the South Atlantic and parts of the South Indian Ocean is transmitted from Cape Town, South Africa, and for the eastern part of the South Indian Ocean it comes from the radio station of Perth. In telegraphy mode (Morse code transmission), there is less chance of misunderstanding or misinterpretation in heavy radio traffic, and the available information is more professional than that from the chains operated by hams. Taking the daily Morse notes also saved energy, as my set was only in the receiving mode.

The radio traffic in the air above the oceans was huge. Much news and information reached me that was not closely connected with my situation, but I listened anyway because it was interesting. In addition to information about the weather, sea state, route of icebergs, and so on, the coast stations also gave up-to-date information on buoys, lighthouses, floating debris, the coordinates of submarines, naval exercises, research vessels, drilling platforms, meteorological rockets observed, and even incidences of pirate attacks.

In the Roaring Forties, there was very little chance of meeting another vessel, and I hoped that the icebergs wouldn't float up to my latitude. As for collisions, my primary concerns were lost containers and whales. Meeting one of the larger sea mammals would endanger even a boat twice *Salammbo*'s size. As previously mentioned, there had been disquieting news about the number of yachts sunk by whales increasing each year. This in part stemmed from the happy news that whales, protected in many waters, had increased in number and would therefore be encountered more often. It would take quite a whale to sink *Salammbo*, but breaking off the rudder or wind vane would be devastating enough.

But there were no signs of whales around *Salammbo*. In the last days of October I had to fight not whales but the waves that were battering *Salammbo* like bulldozers.

EXCERPTS FROM THE LOG
October 25, 1990

I had my first accident. I hurt myself. The day started out all wrong, with one storm after another since dawn. They came in brief intervals from all directions, and I couldn't figure out which way to run. That was why I started to make more mistakes. While performing maintenance on a winch, I lost an irreplaceable pawl. Not long after that I tore one of my jibs to pieces.

I was angry, and everything I did upset me more. I found it insulting that my chart, based on an 1886 survey, showed Austria where Hungary was. I had not noticed it before, even though I had handled the chart often.

I heard on the radio that Nandi Fa had arrived in good shape at Cape Town. I was relieved, for I had been concerned when he had to go through the perils of the Atlantic Ocean, keeping a good position in the BOC field. Then my jealousy got the better of me—he would have all the earthly pleasures, safety, festivities, warm food, and to top it off, a mug of beer.

At 1900 hours, I was in the cabin when a fast approaching roar suppressed the fortissimo of the raging sea. I guessed that it was not the Orient Express approaching, and my ever dangerous curiosity led me to open the companionway hatch. I shouldn't have done that.

When I spotted the rogue wave towering 15-20 feet over the 40-foot-high regulars, I jerked my head back like a mouse seeing a falcon. Normally I had to turn my head 90 degrees to pull it through the narrow opening of the top hatchboard. But my fright and the automatic reflex to close the hatch did not give me time for that. Hitting the side latch of the board, I tore my upper eyelid. My face was full of blood, as was the range after I crashed onto it, tearing it out of its gimbals.

Stunned from the pain and half-blind from the blood, I felt from the motion of the boat that the giant wave had passed by, barely touching *Salammbo*. Even so, the boat was forced into a submissive prostration. I guessed from the heeling angle that the mast must have touched the water. I searched blindly for the first aid kit, grabbed it from its nook, and bandaged myself quickly. Swaying to and fro, I cleaned up the pools of blood.

The day should be damned when I decided to venture on these crazy waters of the world...

October 30, 1990
Position: 39°08'S and 057°10'E. Heading: 90°. Speed: 6 knots. Wind: Force 8. I sailed 90 n. miles yesterday with a reefed jib.
My torn eyelid healed well. I changed my messy head-covering bandage to a smaller taped one. In the previous days I had only been able to see with one eye because of the bandages, which had disturbed me a lot. Now that I could open both eyes, I felt that I could see more than enough of the ocean with just one.

If I hated anything more than the sea, it was my unkempt appearance and dirtiness. Everything was soggy due to the 70% humidity and the waves that swept over the boat, making it barely tolerable. I could bathe only once every 10 days, not just because of the cold and my constant attention to the boat, but also because my fresh water supply was diminishing. I had to use innovative techniques to bathe head to toe in less than a gallon of water. Nevertheless, I stuck tenaciously to the routine of daily shaving, and only the wildest storms stopped me from brushing my teeth.

One thing more complicated than bathing was the use of the head. I used a seacock to secure the inlet and outlet of the hand-operated unit against the backflow of water. Frequent operation of the pump is well recommended, especially in strong wave motion. There was no chance for quiet meditation in that tiny corner of the boat. Trying to do one's business and acrobatics at the same time is grotesque. But I couldn't find any humor in it.

November 2, 1990
Position: 38°58'S and 064°18'E. Heading: 70°. Speed: 6 knots.
Hellish weather. The wind tried to climb the last rungs of the Beaufort

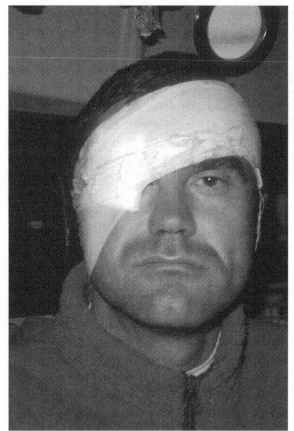

Above: *Bad look after a bad storm: the aftermath of my first accident.*

Scale. Its speed was about 75 knots. This storm was not predicted by any coast station.

The raging of the ocean started at 0100 hours. The whistle of the sudden increase in wind speed made me jump out of my coffin-bunk. In spite of my haste, time seemed to stand still as I struggled just to extricate myself from my bunk, even as the water streamed in through the companionway boards and rushed over my feet. I had pulled a waterproof plastic bag over the bottom part of my sleeping bag. Both had to be discarded before I could pull on the foul weather gear and boots.

Outside, I disengaged the wind vane and tried to balance the wildly dancing boat with everything I had. The ocean looked white in the darkness of the night. The terrifyingly strong pressure of the wind seemed to grind the tops of the 40- to 50-foot-high waves to dust, sending the watery mess onto *Salammbo*. But the worst was yet to come—two dark walls loomed from behind, exceeding the 40-foot-high mast of *Salammbo*. I felt that these were the moments when the helmsman could do only one thing: pray!

The first wave mountain rumbled by like a locomotive. Before I had time for a relieved sigh, the second wave reached *Salammbo*. It broke right behind the boat, and the huge mass of water fell over me and pressed me hard against the wheel. Gasping for air as my head and body were submerged in the water, I suddenly thought that if the wave had broken right over the boat we couldn't have survived it.

The water ran through me in a second, but it filled up the cockpit. I knew the capacity of the cockpit by heart, and that the two tons of water would weigh down the rear end of the boat. I stood up to my waist in the water, clutched the wheel, and waited for the water to pass through the drain holes or splash over the sides of the rolling boat. It lasted for several minutes, but then I saw with great relief that both *Salammbo* and I would be able to go on.

The storm lasted all night and into the next day, prolonging the tension that had coiled up in me. The 80- to 85-knot wind sent the waves higher than the mast by the hundreds and thousands. I needed all my strength to steer *Salammbo* away from the direction of the wind, to keep her broad reaching. After the incident in the night, I was terrified of the possibility of a capsize. I feared that a breaking wave could cause a serious accident. It could be a dismasting, breaking off the rudder, loosening the keel, or even bashing in the hatches and sinking the boat.

By 3:00 in the afternoon I had been standing—or hanging on—in the same way for 15 hours straight, since the cry of the wind had first broken my sleep the night before. The tiredness numbing my muscles was reaching my brain. But after each wave I experienced a strange sensation, in spite of my fears. I was filled with amazement and a feeling of wonderment. Each wave was an obstacle, each climb out of a trough was a fight, but what made it important for me was the spectacle of it all.

The ocean whipped up by the raging storm presented a picture so incredible and astonishing that I would have become a statue transfixed in awe if my body were not forced to follow the wild motion of the boat. The watery walls built over me in seconds, showing the darkest shades of blue. The foam tiles on the roofs of the waves were blown apart after every collapse… up and down, up and down. I had flown into unknown dimensions of highs and lows.

And the sounds! The sounds of rolling waves. I heard their rumbling for miles, and then my pupils and my stomach tightened. The giants of the realm were coming, the stomping of their boots echoing in my ears. When they arrived they ruled the ocean with their 50-60 foot height and wrestled down their smaller subjects with frightening speed.

Then it happened—something I never could have believed. A wave heaved *Salammbo* to its peak, and my moderately fast displacement type boat started to surf on the waves. We didn't fall into the troughs that opened before us like abysses, but slid from wave to wave, faster and faster. I was pressed to the wheel and felt like a spaceman at liftoff. The five-ton boat slid like a surfboard, taking on the 30-40 knot speed of the waves.

The flight lasted for several minutes and I didn't feel us slowing down. Then a "traditional" wave kicked us in the side, indicating that the giants had left the scene. The experience of the express train ride was with me for hours, as if we had transcended space and time. It was frightening and ecstatic, giving me a feeling of wonderment and an unexplainable glory. I saw all of that... nature showed it to me, leaving me as a surviving eyewitness.

November 5, 1990
Position: 39°20'S and 071°53'E. Heading: 100°. Speed: 6 knots. Wind: 35-40 knots westerly. Cloudy sky.
Sailing in storms for weeks had made me so tired that my frayed nerves reacted in an unusual way. I could not sleep, even when I could afford the time. After the long hours spent at the helm, I only had enough strength to stumble down the companionway steps and sit on the lowest one. I had no energy to make the few extra steps to my bunk. I just sat and stared ahead. Other times I sat at the chart table. On the chart of the Indian Ocean, my fingers covered the distance between my actual position and the West Australian port of Fremantle, as if I could hasten my progress towards the faraway shores. I had planned to follow the 40° Latitude until 090-100° East, and then turn towards Australia.

I discovered in the night that my masthead light had broken. Maybe a large bird had smashed into it. It hung by one wire.

I carefully examined every corner of the boat, searching for any possible sources of accidents. If the forces of nature were unleashed, the apparently properly operating instruments and the best of materials could fail or collapse from the overload. Before the last storm, I had gone to adjust the prop shaft into its proper position and discovered to my chagrin that one of the four mounts holding the diesel engine to the stringers was loose. It was terrible even to imagine what a 300 lb. engine could do if it broke free in the hold. I tightened the nuts while hanging upside down in the narrow space. It was an awful job, and it quickly became stiflingly hot in the tight space of the engine room.

I was filled with fear of a fire on board, which is always more serious on the water than on land; there is nowhere to escape when out at sea.   I was always very careful with the propane. I painted both of my tanks with special anti-corrosion paint to prevent cavitation. The tanks were carefully secured outside the cockpit with tubes connecting them to the two-burner stove. The stove was gimbaled and had a flame-out safety valve. Even so, I closed the tank valves after each use and burnt out the gas from the tubing. I tested the conduits and junctions with soapy water and ventilated the bilge once a week. At least I didn't have to worry about electrical fires—my most important instruments, the Sat. Nav., speedometer, etc., had all given up one after the other, and few pieces of equipment remained in working condition.

After the stormy days, I checked the activator of my life raft. Keeping a possible dismasting in mind, I kept my emergency bag beside me. A cable cutter and storm anchor were also close at hand.

While completing all this scrupulous checking I hoped that I was really doing it to prevent any accidents, rather than as a foreboding of something sinister.

November 6, 1990

I had covered 140 n. miles in the previous 24 hours. My concern was not with the distance or the problems with the Force 7-8 wind, but with my own health and nutrition. I like dairy products, but anything that I made out of milk powder upset my stomach. I could not get rid of my nasty cramps, and I was still sure that it was caused by my appendix. The thought of it haunted me.

I sent a message through the Equator radio station to my friends at MAHART: "Send a medical guide to me in Australia." The recipient of this message, Attila Terdi, had done a lot before to help my undertaking. I was sure that he would arrange it in time. Until then I would have to experiment with my menu. For example, in the early morning I tried eating muesli or cereals in lemon juice. One thing that consoled me regarding my health was that, thanks to the vitamin and mineral preparation from Hoffman-LaRoche, I could not find a trace of a problem caused by malnutrition.

In the afternoon the waves threw a squid into the boat. It was dinnertime, so I thought that it was appropriate. I threw back only its head and cleaned the rest. Then I fried the tentacles and the cartilaginous back of the foot-long creature in oil. Unfortunately my fight with the swinging range and the pot of boiling oil was not followed by gastronomic pleasures. The dinner was neither enjoyable nor enough. But the sun came out, so that was something.

November 7, 1990
Position: 39°35'S and 077°22'E.

A new storm came with 60-knot winds. It lasted for hours, and then the wind abated. But it left the big waves as a souvenir. I picked up an Australian radio ham from Perth named Ellen. It was good to chat with an inhabitant of the city that was my goal destination. After the talk I again got the blues, and it started to rain.

According to my chart, I was 60 miles from Amsterdam Island. I knew that a few people lived on the archipelago. But I was in no mood to fish out the pilot book to find out who lived there and what the heck they were doing at the end of the earth.

November 10, 1990
Position: 38°38'S and 082°15'E. Wind: Force 7 gusting 8 southwest. Last day's progress was 115 n. mile.
I had to run out hourly to the cockpit in the stormy weather. If I had known that my Sat. Nav. would die anyway, I would have invested in good foul weather gear instead. The endless dunking and being constantly wet was getting on my nerves.

At least my speedometer worked; it would have been very difficult to get my position without it. To get my DR (dead reckoning) position, I had to consider the following: wind changes, currents, tidal changes, boat speed, and slip, among others. First of all, I had to find a celestial body, but the sun came out only for minutes at a time, and it was a real hunt to spot it.

My attempts to get a fix in the heavy weather were exhausting. It was a miracle that my sextant was not damaged or lost altogether. The sloshing water damaged the surface coating of the mirrors, despite my attempts to wash them in fresh water. Another problem was jotting down the measured data—I couldn't run into the closed cabin every minute, and it is difficult to write in the wind and the hail. Finally I devised a solution. I hung a plastic board on a string around my neck and used a felt marking pen to write down the data. After each measurement I cleaned the board with spirit. The sight reduction wasn't easy either. I could lock out the wind and waves from inside the cabin, but not the motion. Handling the tables and constructing the plot required all my patience.

That day I was lucky and got the sun. At least I knew where I was, even if it was not where I wanted to be.

November 14, 1990
Position: 38°48'S and 090°16'E. Heading: 110°. Temperature: 14° C (57° F). For the first time in several days, I could write down that the sea state was moderate. I couldn't remember how long it had been since *Salammbo* had sailed with its working sails and the sun had been shining. Capitalizing on that uncommon occasion, I permitted myself a rare luxury by bathing in several liters of water. After shaving, I stroked my smooth face with satisfaction. I tried to do everything fast; I had the feeling that it would not last.

November 15, 1990

My prediction came true. Since dawn the wind had been Force 7-9, turning into northwest-southwest. The rain was pouring down. I tried to call Paul (VK6PY), a Perth ham, on the radio. I knew that he was also in the Merchant Marine, serving on 5,000-ton and bigger ships. I couldn't find out more; stratospheric disturbances prevented our aerial meeting. My anger about this failure was increased by my renewed stomach problems.

November 17, 1990

I could only guess my position: 39°40'S and 097°27'E. The sun shot was not successful, and the sextant was soaked. The weather had become rough. The barometer, which was at a low of 99.3 kPa, fell to 98.6. Within two hours the wind rose again to the upper grades of the Beaufort Scale: storm force 10-11.

In the afternoon it worsened. The showers rushed after each other and a veritable flood was coming down on *Salammbo*. The rain was not falling or pouring, but coming in a deluge as if the skies had broken. It reminded me of the worst tropical rains, which were not unusual in that region. The waves blew over *Salammbo* every second or so, and water poured on the inside and outside of my useless foul weather gear. I felt like the 85-knot wind was tearing my bones within it.

When I thought that I could leave the boat to the wind vane I pressed myself in through the companionway, but inside I had another cause for worry. The propane tank was empty and I had to change it. To do that I had to climb back into the cockpit, fish out the new tank, and change the connections. I tried to pry the tank from the lazarette beside the wheel. My fingers were so stiff from the cold that I dropped the pressure regulator into the hold. It was impossible to find it amidst the heaped up stores, and the waves started to flood the hold. I banged down the hatch and wanted to scream. The lack of propane meant that in this terrible cold I couldn't even make warm tea or soup. I scratched out a soy slice and went back to the wheel chewing it angrily.

Nothing changed for the evening. One cloudburst followed the other. Taller and taller waves were built by the never abating winds. At the agreed time I sat down at the radio to make contact with the Equator station. On the arranged frequency there was only deafening noise and interference coming from the set. I was sure that Zsolt Pal and Karoly Nyemcsek were trying just as hard, but I could not hear their voices. I didn't give up. Wedging myself in place with my legs I tried again, but to no avail. The awful weather must have mixed up the airwaves. I tried again. I called Perth in Australia, but the result was the same. The failure made me depressed. It was the first day since Gibraltar that I had been unable to talk to my friends.

I fought back to the wheel in the rain and waves. It was now 70 hours that I had been on my feet, and after midnight I felt that I could not go on. I engaged the wind vane and climbed into the cabin. Shivering, I pulled the sleeping bag over me. To cheer myself up I fantasized that Australia was only 1,000 miles away.

UNDER THE BLOWS OF WAVES

A horrendous crash—as if my eardrums were splintering. At the same time I felt my body hit the cabin ceiling. As I fell back, my clearing mind realized that we had capsized. It was interesting that apart from the big bang, the worst thing was to be startled out of sleep. One can get used to the feeling of fear on the Southern Ocean, but a sudden alarm can disable.

Even then my reactions were quite quick. Still numb from the knock on my head, I pushed myself out of the coffin-bunk, not even trying to get out of the sleeping bag. I hopped to the chart table as if in a cocoon. First I switched on the deck headlight. I hung on with one hand as the boat started to right itself. My first thought was wondering if the keel had broken off, so I switched on the bilge pump automatically. A faint light came into the cabin, and the first thing I noticed were the shards of my favorite thick-walled mug on the chart table. I grabbed my flashlight. I didn't know whether there was any water coming in, but I was deeply concerned about the condition of the cockpit and deck. Directing the lamp through the translucent hatchboard I saw the stump of the wind vane, showing that the boat was wallowing on the waves without steering.

I tore off my sleeping bag and grabbed my oilies and boots. A glance at my watch showed it was 0145 hours—scarcely an hour and a half since I had left the helm. I grabbed the pipe wrench from its place at the table leg and ran for the spare wind vane blade.

As I opened the hatch I felt the gale's saltwater in my eyes. At that point I was unable to estimate the damage caused by the capsize. The first thing was to get the new blade on and make sure the wind vane was operating properly. When it was ready to work again, I switched it off and hung on the wheel in order to turn *Salammbo* back to her course and stop the crazy dancing.

I was afraid that the mighty knockdown could have dismasted the boat. Fighting the wheel, I aimed my flashlight straight ahead. Relief. The light was reflected by the metal of the still-standing mast. The wind had torn off the masthead light, which was hanging on its wire, but the jib was still held tight in the 75-knot wind. I noticed that the wind speed sensor had disappeared and only the frame was left of the dodger. The light of my lamp was not enough to see whether my lashed down sails were still on deck. I would see to that in the morning.

I could not do any more outside, so I left the boat to the wind vane and squeezed myself back into the cabin. When I stepped on the floor I could feel myself trembling. The lights worked, the batteries had not broken loose, but everything else was in terrible shape. On the floor, the cooking oil from the broken bottle mixed with honey and ketchup, and in the middle of the slimy mess lay my clothing. I blessed my providence that the utensils and other hard objects had been solidly fastened. I noticed that only my pencils and compasses had been strewn about. Since I saw no water coming in, I switched off the bilge pump. I did not notice the time, so I cannot say how much time passed between the knockdown and the damage assessment. I looked at the cabin with desperation and tried to regain my nerves.

DANGERS OF MY DREAMS

When I went back to the wheel I felt I would collapse from the leaden tiredness, but on that night I would certainly not get back into my coffin-bunk.

The storm lasted until morning and showed no sign that it was losing any strength. Although I had been near it all night, I noticed only then that the 8-foot radio antenna fastened to the pulpit had been bent by the water's hammering. My attention went to the propane system. I tried to find the regulator. I would have given anything for a cup of hot tea. After opening the hatch, I had a new reason to hurry. Propane had poured out into the lazarette.[44] After performing a quick fitting and changing of the air with the hand pump, I was good for only two things: crying and swearing.

In the afternoon I steered the boat with numbed ingrained motions, from wave top to wave top. The force 10-11 wind blew my head clear.

The capsize had been caused by my impatience. I had tried to hurry, but I should have changed down my 120-square-foot reefed jib. There was no legitimate excuse for not putting on the 80-square-foot German jib (which I had thought not to be strong enough), or the 60-square-foot storm jib (which I had feared would slow down my progress). It was a mistake in the west-northwest wind to try to keep an easterly course. I should have deviated from the direction of the waves by reaching or broad reaching.

I had been sailing the seas for 6 months since my start from Pola, and on that night I could not suppress my desire for speed, to get to port sooner. One thing came more clearly to my mind: Australia was still one thousand miles away. But after I had already sailed immense distances, this continent seemed to be so near. The imagined victory of this land had given me a false sense of security.

I meditated for hours about the circumstances of the capsize, imagining

---

[44] The lazarette is an area on a boat used for storage.

the huge wave that had caught the boat broadside. Judging from the trajectory of the spilled items, I estimated that the mast must have had a 130-140° tilt—that is, 40-50° below sea level. I imagined what could have happened if the keel had broken off, or if the wave had broken in through port lights or hatches, or if the boat had not rolled, but had pitch-poled, and drifted dismasted towards Antarctica.

Fortunately the actual situation—if not consoling—was less terrifying, and brought my thoughts back to the boat. I started cleaning up the gooey mess from the floor.

At 1400 hours local time, 9 in the morning at home, I got in touch with the Equator station. Zsolt Pal was at the set and the transmission was good. I told the tale of the previous night to Zsolt, who immediately grabbed the phone. I knew that Jozsi Gal, who was preparing for his five-year-long circumnavigation (cruising around the globe with his family), had his hands full building his boat, but that he would still hurry to the Oreghegy station when he heard about my capsize.[45]

A one-hour discussion followed. I told him the story in detail. We went into every technical aspect of it, and it was a good feeling to tell my woes to somebody who understood. He and Nandi Fa had survived an Indian Ocean capsize on their voyage with *St. Jupat*. We agreed that during a long voyage serious accidents very often happen near land, probably triggered by impatience. I listened carefully to Jozsi's calm advice. In the meantime I talked the tension out of myself.

In the evening I arranged everything very carefully and decided that no matter what, I would lie down, even if for just a couple of hours. And then I slept, just slept.

---

[45] The reader may wonder why Jozsi Gal's circumnavigation would take as long as five years, but the difference is that his was to include many long-term stops along the way.

7

THE HARBOR OF SAFETY AND DOUBTS: FREMANTLE
(1990 November 19 — December 19)

"This above all: to thine own self be true,
And it must follow, as the night the day,
Thou canst not then be false to any man."
　　　　　　　—William Shakespeare, *Hamlet*

IN THE COMING DAYS I TRIED TO GET AWAY FROM THE Roaring Forties, and sailed farther up north according to the original plan. The relatively fast progress was aided by the steady Force 8 southwest wind. I could tell from the weather report of the Perth radio that I had just avoided a very nasty storm center, but I was preoccupied by the disorder in the cabin. The cleaning up and washing and drying of my clothes required many hours of work every day. The biggest problem was that I had no intact outfit left that I could put on under the foul weather gear, except for one that I had intended to wear for special occasions onshore. Having no other solution, I had to put on my festive white pants and fashionable navy blue pullover. No doubt I was the best dressed sailor who ever sailed the Roaring Forties.

ON STORMY CORRIDORS
On the 22nd of November, as I reached 35° South Latitude, the weather miraculously changed. The wind abated, and the temperature went up to 20° C (68° F). It was most pleasant to bask in the sun. Stretching out in the

Above: *Trying to dry everything off after the capsize.*

cockpit, I let the warmth go through my bones. After all those numbingly cold days and nights, it was an amazing sensation. The wind fell to a breeze, no screaming, only peace and quiet. The slow plodding started to make me nervous after a couple of days because the wind vane cannot operate in light winds, and I cannot do much with hand steering either. Yet the shore kept calling me.

The 25th of November was a day of imaginary festivities. A year ago, on a cool autumn day, had been the christening of *Salammbo*. I recalled the ceremony when Janos Csoma, the priest of Almadi, had blessed *Salammbo*, and we had recited the Lord's Prayer together with our friends and guests.

To help the celebration, dolphins appeared around the boat and conversed with their whistling sounds. I had guests from above too, but instead of the albatrosses, they were birds with flapping, colorful wings. They were truly emissaries of land.

A less festive happening of the day was the wind springing up and turning. I also found that my fresh water supply was out. I only had some

Above: *The SOUL of any boat is her name—*
Salammbo's christening ceremony, Balatonalmadi, 1989.

bottled mineral water left.

In the next two days I passed 33° South and 110° East. According to my calculations I was 270 n. miles away from the Australian shores, which I could reach in 3 days if everything went well. The weather didn't think so, as it sent a nasty gale into the area with headwinds. On the 26th I had some excitement. The radio at Perth had been giving daily shipping reports of dense sea traffic, which gave me a strange feeling, as I had not seen any ships for months. Well, I still didn't see a ship, but a passenger plane showed up. Its pilot could probably hardly see me, but I was waving happily at the first conveyance I had seen in a very long time.

The closeness of the shore was indicated by the good reception of the Perth stations on the AM bands. I was fascinated by the easy style of the interviewers, who called the politicians by their first names as they pressed them with the hardest of questions. One program discussed the environment, and whether it was better to sell milk in glass bottles. There was a lot of light and classical music, and I noticed that the announcer of the latter was named John Kadar—certainly of Hungarian descent. I was touched when the first Christmas carols were broadcast.

EXCERPTS FROM THE LOG
November 28, 1990

The wind strengthened to Force 7-8 during the morning. One reefing eye tore out, and the wind blew my sunglasses into the sea. The day started out well otherwise, and Fremantle Harbor was not too far away. I had only a large scale chart of the coast and I studied it for days, but I could not get far with it. Navigation in this area is dangerous; one has to find the right corridor snaking between coral heads. It was never so important to have a correct navigational fix. But the bad weather and clouds made the measurements uncertain, and as the boat was driven faster and faster, I felt less and less comfortable.

As in all critical situations, the Great Caretaker helped out. The skies cleared in the afternoon, and as a rare gift I was able to shoot the sun and moon at the same time. I had the fix—my position was 32°19'S and 115°04'E. The harbor was 40 miles away on a heading of 60°. "Hurrah, I can moor today!" I thought. My imagination took wing. I saw myself under a hot shower that day, and the next day in a restaurant with a huge mug of beer.

The Indian Ocean wind crossed out my calculations in a minute. The gale built taller and taller waves under the boat. Where did it come from? Naturally, from dead ahead. Instead of the hot shower, I got a cold shower. There would be no docking today.

After a brief rest, at 2100 hours local time, I went on deck. At 60° magnetic on the compass there was the blinking of the lighthouses at Rottnest Island, visible for 26 miles. Right on time, where and when I calculated. I was overwhelmed. I had not seen land for three and a half months, and the extraordinary accuracy of my navigation counts as my greatest success in this trade. My self-presented badge of honor made me so happy that I would have danced on the deck if my limbs were not nailed down by tiredness.

Rottnest Island is 12 miles from the mainland. I could reach the harbor in only three hours. But I repressed the temptation. My memory was still fresh with the recent repercussions of my impatience. Without a detailed chart or a working depth sounder, it would be too chancy to go among the rocks. I resigned myself to prepare for the night and hove the boat to. I tied the reefed main to the center, and set the jib and rudder to windward. The slow forereaching would see us through the night, and I could have some rest. The maneuver was not without danger, for if the wind turned, it could push the boat onto the rocks. But the ocean could not be so malevolent in the last hours…

Trusting my luck, I climbed into my sleeping bag.

November 29, 1990

At 3:00 in the morning, it was already daylight and the wind was abating. At sunrise, I blessed my carefulness in stopping the boat. The sight in front of me was terrifying. The blue waves of the ocean broke over sharp rocks and numerous corals. If I had continued at night, I would have smashed the boat on them.

At 8:00 in the morning something fantastic happened. I saw the first human—only fleetingly, because he sped by on his luxury yacht—but he waved to me with a smile. The contours of the shore and Fremantle showed more clearly. In my euphoria I took a picture of every single insignificant rock. I got hold of myself, and once the wind dissipated in the sun, I started to clean up and wash. I would be the first Hungarian sailor to tie up in Fremantle, so I had to watch my appearance.

After cleaning the boat I organized myself. A shave, hair wash, and manicure were in order. I looked at myself incredulously in the taped-together mirror. There were white hairs I had not seen before, deeper wrinkles, and a new scar on my left eyelid. But I was still alive, and the harbor was only 2 miles away. One more important task: the Hungarian flag had to go on the backstay, and on the starboard flag halyard, for lack of an Australian, went the British courtesy flag. On the port halyard went the 150-year-old pennant of the National Boating Association (Nemzeti Hajos Egylet). Decked out in flags, *Salammbo* slid easily towards the shore.

A fishing boat returning from the ocean came abreast. To my amazement the crew greeted me. I didn't understand their singular helpfulness, but when they offered to guide me to Success Harbor I happily accepted. Then I realized—the barnacles. The waterline of *Salammbo* was covered by those 3- to 4-inch-long creatures. With my stores used up, the boat rode higher, and their great numbers were visible. This covering had grown in tropical waters, and it told the whole story to the experienced fishermen.

Our paths diverged at the mouth of the harbor. They went to the fishing harbor, but pointed us towards a forest of masts. The breakwater was built of huge stone blocks, and when I moved into the protected waters a miracle happened. The sea turned as smooth as if it had been ironed, and for the first time in months, *Salammbo* floated horizontally. It was the end of the ceaseless dancing and grabbing, and I could safely put a glass on the table. My awe over that then turned to absolute wonderment. I was astonished by the size of the harbor. Success Harbor is a port of nearly one and a half thousand yachts.

Trying to find a slip, I tied up at the nearby fuel dock. A chap in overalls caught the docking line and asked, "Where from?" He looked incredulous at my answer, but warned me, "Don't step ashore before the officials arrive."

In spite of that I tried to get to shore anyway, and my helper kindly recorded it on the camcorder. For the first few steps, walking felt like stepping off an escalator in ski boots.

Since Gibraltar, I had covered the 14,000 n. miles to Australia in 123 days and one hour.

HAPPINESS

Sunshine, bright clear colors, soft onshore breeze. Waiting on deck, I was in a state of weightlessness. The idyllic feeling lasted until Chris Mews, the harbormaster, arrived in his launch.

The pleasant tanned man in white shorts, knee socks, freshly ironed shirt, and bush hat reminded me of the elegant officers of colonial days. He examined *Salammbo* expertly, and I knew that he could tell the trials we had gone through, despite the cosmetic spruce-up of the boat and myself. Later I learned that he had participated six times in the Sydney Hobart race, which is rarely run without the loss of a boat.

Following his launch, we proceeded to the heart of the harbor, where we were greeted by the reception committee. Instead of well-wishers it was the uniformed army of immigration, customs, and health officials. I had the privilege of enjoying their polite but thorough interrogation for three hours. During this time I answered countless questions and filled out forms. Chris excused these, explaining the special insular position of the country and the importance of its protection. I was not surprised; I had endured a similar procedure when visiting Australia in 1987 for the America's Cup. That time I had lost, with a heavy heart, a quarantined salami. Now I happily relinquished the awful powdered milk and the cans of peach-flavored fish not yet donated to the seagulls.

It wasn't the end. Two hefty, stern looking guys with a huge peaceful looking dog occupied the cabin. I like dogs, even drug detecting ones, but not dog hair. Yet the good animal was even more apprehensive than me of the inspection. The poor 'sniffer' was trembling in the small cabin, apparently on its first official visit on a small bobbing watercraft.

After a quick mugshot, I was given my cruising permit. It was late afternoon and I was automatically estimating the elevation and azimuth of the sun and moon when they bade me a friendly goodbye. Waiting for their cue, a new crowd of visitors arrived. Chris gathered the skippers of the other boats in the harbor to my boat. The old salts understood my impatience, congratulated me, offered their help, and departed. One named Peter Fletcher invited me for dinner. I realized later why his name seemed familiar—from the Mutiny on the Bounty.

Finally left alone, I had a few exciting moments. I started toward the harbor's showers with slow measured steps, swaying a bit, avoiding people, managing to knock over only a trash can and a bike rack. I stood for a long time under the hot shower, but I couldn't fully enjoy it. My water-saving habits were so ingrained that I was bothered by the freely flowing stream.

Nor did I waste a drop of the ice-cold Australian beer presented by Chris after my shower. The official of the harbor considerately loaned me a hundred dollars, explaining that the banks were closed. The West Australians are openhearted and friendly, and the harbor, despite its mammoth size, had a family atmosphere about it. In the central building were the reception area, cafeteria, restaurant, bar, shops, club lounges, and toilets. The repair facilities were farther away. The slips had access fingers, electricity, water, and a telephone every 50 feet. The doors were opened by magnetic access cards, and trolleys were provided for supplies. It was modern, clean, and well-kept, and I was impressed by the jolly company during my walkabout.

It was time for the first friendly dinner. I was afraid that my hunger-incited eagerness would make me a spectacle, but I succeeded in putting away all the offered meats, sweets, and fruits without creating a show. The most interesting member of the company was Michel. He was a retired French fighter pilot, about 60 years old but looking 40, who had decided after retirement to sail around the world. He had started out on his beautiful 46-foot ketch from Brazil, and after a stop in Cape Town, had arrived in Fremantle two weeks before. Like me, he also had capsized in the Indian Ocean. But his boat had the latest equipment, satellite navigation, radar, autopilot, and air conditioning, and the damage sustained was more serious than *Salammbo*'s. Michel planned to set sail in two weeks to round Cape Horn in the most favorable season. He was the first French acquaintance I had liked instantly, and our friendship grew deeper during our short Australian visit.

New visitors brought me happy feelings. László Csaba—who until recently had been president of the Hungarian House in Perth—and his wife had looked for me following the news from home. They invited me to their house for the St. Nicholas feast. For a come-from-afar sailor it was very pleasant to meet compatriots, and so I happily accepted. Then I hurried to the phone to tell my father first about my arrival. At home it was about dawn, but sleep was washed out of his eyes by his tears of joy.

Going back to *Salammbo*, I retired and enjoyed the unusual quiet. "Sleeping like a log" was never so well applied a phrase as it was to me on this night. They could have taken the mast from over my head without me knowing the difference. I was surprised in the morning how the routine of hourly waking and lookouts could be erased in the course of a single night.

Waking up brought a surprise: the gift from Santa Claus. A box waited for me in the cockpit containing milk, eggs, rolls, fruits, chocolate, and other goodies. I started on a long dreamt of 3-minute egg when Chris arrived. It was he who had brought the package, made up by his wife. Over tea we discussed the lifting out, painting, and repairing of *Salammbo*, and the expected expenses. Contrary to his advice, I asked for a slip close to the entrance and reception area, expecting a lot of phone calls. I slid into the Number 1 slip of the 1,500-boat marina.

S.O.S. TO MY FRIENDS

I went to work immediately. First I took the salt off *Salammbo*, which was followed by cleaning and washing all inside spaces. All the things I had believed lost—toothbrush, broken alarm clock, and various utensils—surprisingly appeared. I had to liberate some from the prison of honey or jam. Work was interrupted frequently by phone calls and visitors. My helpful supporters, the Ganz-Danubius Trading Company, sent me good news. A Number 5 reefable jib was underway from Hong Kong. They would also send a masthead light, cordage, and money.

I gave a phone interview to Hungarian Radio's program "During the Day," which had been a faithful follower of my and *St. Jupat*'s voyages. I was contacted by the Hungarian radio station in Sydney, where Miklós Soos showed interest in my voyage.

Just as the number of phone calls increased, so did the number of visitors. It was a frustrating situation, for if nobody had cared it would have been a problem; but if too many came, how could I get ready for the second—and probably more difficult—part of the voyage? In addition to the Australian sailors, more and more Hungarians from Perth looked me up, offering their help and issuing many invitations for the St. Nicholas evening.

We went to the Hungarian House in Uncle Laci's car. The House had been built in the fifties or sixties in a quiet suburban neighborhood, reminding me of our family homes in Hungary. I was received in rich Hungarian by some mature ladies, who immediately put a bowl of gulyas soup into my hands. There were about seventy people around the prepared tables. Sitting among them, I took in the soup—and homesickness. Aunt Ella read my thoughts with the infallible sense of a grandmother and brought me cottage cheese pasta (túrós csusza) with wine.

When the tables were cleared the festive show started. Everybody turned toward the Christmas tree. Santa Claus in his heavy costume spoke with the good language of a country teacher, but it was a pity that some of the children spoke only English. The situation is difficult in many mixed marriages, but a more diligent maintenance of our language would befit the Rakoczi picture and ornate flag of the Hungarian House. I learned later that they had remained Hungarian in every other sense, despite the strong local influence. As in the homeland, they are in diverging factions.

Among the number of my helpers and supporters were those 10-15 persons I remember gratefully for their golden hearts and friendship.

On December 2, my Santa Claus was the Boeing pilot who carried my wife and daughter to me. Our embraces dissolved the tensions of many months of worry.

Salammbo became a family craft for 3 weeks, though I couldn't perform any magic with the tight quarters to make it a true family nest. Even before putting the water and food supplies aboard for the coming journey, the boat was already full of sails, tools, and equipment, not to mention the elbow room needed for the ongoing work. My angels, in order not to be underfoot, spent the first 3 days in the laundry, cleaning my half-year-old dirties with great patience. Our Australian and Hungarian friends saw the situation and organized programs for the ladies, and I worked doubly hard so that we could spend the evenings together.

After the haul-out, I cleaned the bottom of the boat and we repainted it with a better anti-fouling paint (aka "bottom paint"). The electrical conduits were changed in the mast, and a new masthead light and wind gauge were fitted. In anticipation of similar occasions we fastened fold-down steps on the mast. Five torn sails had to be mended and I needed a new dodger. The winches and the wind vane had to be maintained, and the lost rings and pawls replaced.

I changed the sacrificial zincs under the waterline, as well as the shaft and damaged blades of the wind generator. I bought new blades as well. The steering column needed a supporting bracket, and the steering compass light was changed and its cover desalted.

The most important improvements were the satellite navigator, repairs to the speedometer and wind instruments, and mounting the depth gauge transmitter through the hull. The range top received new and stronger pot retainers, and the split Lewmar hatch was given new hinges.

The diesel motor received a full service and a few parts were exchanged. I had to buy charts, cordage, watertight containers, diesel, propane tanks, and a thousand other small but essential things. The question was: with what would I pay for it?

My sponsors helped in this desperate situation. The bosses of the Hungarian Credit Bank knew well that their financial help was not just part of an extraordinary sporting undertaking, but literally a vital contribution. Risk taking is part of banking, but it multiplies in the case of such events. Despite knowing this, the bank stood by me, understanding that their partner was going to risk his life in the coming 30,000 miles. My other sponsors, the Ganz-Danubius Trading Company, knew from their shipping experience the dangers that come with lacking even minimal technical equipment. Faxes came and went, and thanks to Kereskeden Kft, the requested equipment started to arrive. Obtaining reliable navigational equipment meant very expensive purchases, and *Salammbo* had just barely more than the minimum quality equipment. I could not have purchased the most important items, or paid for the yard work, if my wife had not brought loans from my friends with her. I knew that these loans were more than we could carry, and that I would face big problems back home, but here I had to concentrate on the task at hand. I have to admit that the thought of fulfilling my obligations at home weighed on me during those days of preparation.

I thought that *Salammbo*'s preparations were on track, and that the planned departure date of December 29 could be kept. Then new storm clouds gathered—not over the sea, but over me. Organizing food supplies. We made plans with the Quartermaster General's Staff that they were going to assemble all the supplies for the second part. While I was on the Indian Ocean, we had finalized and corrected the contents of the packages via the radio. Major László Dan and Judit Bataszeki had worked on this program with such expertise that it seemed to be the safest part of the resupply. Unfortunately one problem was left unsolved: how to get it all to Perth. We both trusted the promises to cover the costs of airfreight. Sometimes written commitments get "overlooked," and promises are just that. The once enthusiastic promises were taken back, telephones were not answered, and no airfreight outfit could be found to help us. The Quartermaster's experts (of the Hungarian Army), my friends at the Hungarian radio, and my relatives all tried to get it arranged, working day and night for a week, but to no avail. There I stood with a fully prepared boat and only a few cans of leftover food for a half-year voyage.

I had no other option but to do what I had tried to do in Gibraltar: sell my spare radio set. I figured that I could afford the supplies with about 2,000 Australian dollars, and that what I got for the radio could partially cover it. The Australian hams who I asked for help with my plan were taken aback, and started a collection on my behalf. I felt very uncomfortable when the first Austral-Hungarian, Bela Boros, sent a check, and the sailors—with their customary tact—started a collection around the harbor. Never before had I asked for or accepted charitable donations. If I were to start on some work in the harbor I could earn the money in a month, but then my rounding of Cape Horn would be in the most dangerous season. Seeing the difficulty of my situation, the local Hungarians decided to help two days before the start. After a hurried supermarket session we loaded bags and boxes of food into *Salammbo*.

HOLIDAY WITH FAREWELL

The soothing presence of my wife and daughter, and the busy schedule of my friends, helped ensure that I did not become a nervous wreck like I had on the Indian Ocean. Our best memories of Perth were also tied to sailing. The Club organized races every Wednesday and Saturday. The Wednesday races were the family type round-the-buoy ones. But the Saturday ones, which were open to non-racers as well, were hard-fought events— dismastings, collisions, and accidents were commonplace. I participated in several of those races, not with the land-locked *Salammbo* but with an agile New Zealand boat. The boat belonged to my new friend John, and we helmed it together. We succeeded in being within the first five in all the races we entered, even coming first once. The Commodore asked me to present the trophies and give an impromptu description of my experiences. Speaking in front of 250-300 expert sailors was even more exciting than doing so later in the governor's mansion in Perth.

I had accepted an honored invitation to this high-ranking edifice. The Premier of Western Australia held a reception for the representation of ethnic groups, and as a guest from far away I would exchange a few words with these sympathetic politicians. This was one of the rare occasions when I could get into the nearby metropolis, though Perth and its environs deserve a visit. The vast city, lying on scattered hills, is cut into two by the Swan River. The downtown area with its commerce, traffic, and skyscrapers is typical of a large city, while the suburbs show peaceful affluence.

Writing about Perth and the river brings me back to water and boats. I was most proud of my daughter Piroska's participation in the Optimist races of the Royal Perth Freshwater Yacht Club. She showed that she could achieve in Australian waters the same as what she could in the Balaton, earning second and third place finishes in the field.

Time was flying by, and soon Christmas arrived. The warm summer weather, the abundant greenness, and the flowers of the parks didn't remind me of the atmosphere of Christmas at home—but holidays live inside us. I hurriedly finished the work before Christmas Eve in time to get to Perth and buy a modest present for my daughter before closing time. On the way home, for the first time in my life, I cut a lovely branch from a living fir tree. The official of the Hungarian House, Gyuri Vajda, surprised us with tree decorations, turning the fir bough into a true Christmas tree in *Salammbo*'s cabin. In the small cabin we sat around the boat's nicest decoration holding each other's hands. A festive dinner waited for us in the Club's dining room.

Over Christmas the majority of yacht owners went on a cruise, visiting one or more romantic islands. The harbormaster stayed home and invited my family for the Christmas Day dinner. We discovered with surprise that under the tree in their elegant house were presents for us too. Chris demonstrated his practical sense here; a good part of the packages were goodies for my voyage. It was my honor to carve the turkey at the family dinner.

One of our most cherished memories was the evening of the second day of Christmas when one friend, Gyuri Vajda, organized an extraordinary concert in front of the governor's palace in Perth. We sat on blankets in the park along with several thousand others listening to the candlelit carol concert.

The holidays were soon over for us, though most Australians don't return to work until the New Year. The thought of separation cast a shadow on our celebrations, and our forebodings were not dispelled by my

Above: *Unforgettable Christmas Eve with my wife, Zsuzsa...*

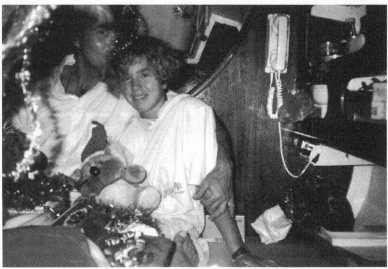

Above: *...And my daughter, Piroska.*

family's participation in the franticness of the last days. With bags in our hands we ran around the markets as well as the mineral water and juice factories. The purchases filled Peter's truck.

On December 27, one day before my departure, my daughter and wife flew home. My unfinished projects prevented me from accompanying them to the airport. As I organized the pile of stores, loneliness again overwhelmed me while I contemplated the uncertainty of ever meeting my family again. But I had to go on.

After biking to the gas station I had another unpleasant surprise—they could not fill the gas cylinders I had from home. I tried other places, but in vain. Finally, I ordered a local cylinder. Naturally, this one did not fit the locker, so I had to change it for two smaller ones. It was late at night when the mounting and plumbing of the bottles was finished. At that moment I had an urge to test it with matches rather than soapy water. The arrangement was disappointing. For the remaining voyage, which would be longer than the first leg, I only had one 3-kilogram cylinder and one 4-kilogram cylinder instead of my own 11-kilogram bottle.

Above: *All of my provisions on the dock, waiting to be crammed into Salammbo for the second—and longer—leg of the journey. Also visible here is the new white dodger I had to buy in Australia, since the blue one was wrecked after the capsize.*

By 3:00 in the morning on December 29, just about everything was on board. It was difficult to maneuver in the crowded cabin. An unfortunate move caused some liquid from a leaking can to burn my hand. Gyuri Vajda tried to find me some baking soda while I continued the fight with the containers.

The first visitors appeared at the crack of dawn, followed by an uninterrupted stream of more well-wishers. When I motored to the fuel dock, I did not notice that the poop deck of *Salammbo* was under the high dock wall, and I accidentally frayed the antenna connection of the new Sat. Nav. as a result.

My compatriots were looking out for my needs, and when I said that I could use some old tires, Sandor Jandrasek put some on my deck in short order. I planned to use them as drogues in the region of Cape Horn. Back at my slip I had started for the showers for my last freshwater soaking, when I met Uncle Laci Csaba. He was pushing a cart full of Aunt Ella's baked creations. I started to feel lonesome again.

Back at the boat, my friends and acquaintances who had come to say farewell filled up the pier. The local sailors were sitting around on the concrete, and even the children talked quietly. My Hungarian friends were in a good mood and presented me with a Walker taffrail log. The cabin had changed in my short absence; mementos, good luck charms, drinks, books, and other presents were heaped on the table. When László Csada stepped into the cabin and put the sign of the cross on my forehead, I could not stop my tears.

Fortunately the TV crew arrived, and their usual routine stopped my melancholy. Using this time, I quickly bade goodbye with handshakes and embraces. The Australians went to their boats to form an escort. The boat parade was headed by the harbor rescue ship, followed by Chris on the Commander's launch. Behind them was a 60-foot two-master, and then the 46-foot *Rebecca Jane*. On the smallest boat, the 30-foot *Perfect Balance*, Laci Csada and Gyuri Vajda—my best Australian friends—were crowded between John Showel and Peter Fletcher.

The sea was rolling bigger and bigger toward us as we pulled away from the harbor, and the wind had picked up too. The boats followed me for 12 miles and then started to peel off. I was waving for several minutes before I climbed down into my heaving cabin and started to cry.

Above: *Onward to the Pacific Ocean: my departure from Australia, as captured from one of the escort boats, December 1990.*

8

RACE TO SURVIVE ON THE PACIFIC OCEAN
(1990 December 30 — 1991 February 24)

"Only someone who has nothing to lose has nothing to fear. I am said to seek death. Absurd. I worship life, and the dangers are only one way for me to give reason and direction to my life."

—Gil Delmar

ONCE AGAIN I HAD AN IMMENSE DISTANCE IN FRONT OF ME. According to my planned route I was to sail in the Indian Ocean for a while, then reach down towards the 50° S. Latitude. I would round Tasmania's South East Cape. Leaving New Zealand's South West Cape behind, I would then cross the Pacific Ocean before reaching the highlight of the voyage: South America's southernmost point, Cape Horn.

Leaving the western shore of Australia behind, I felt that my timing would place me at that feared meeting point of the Pacific and Atlantic Oceans in early March. If I survived it, many thousands of miles then waited for me on the Atlantic to Gibraltar. My planned arrival at the gates of the Mediterranean was the end of May. It seemed to be infinitely far off. My arrival at Pola should coincide with my starting date of June 16, one year's difference.

A Force 7 gale drove me on to the Indian Ocean and 1991. The four weeks spent on land had taken away my sea legs. My tiredness was capped with seasickness. In this state, I did not find it funny when the line of a fishing buoy wrapped itself around my rudder. Fighting the seasickness, and well anchored to the boat, I dived in with a big kitchen knife to solve the

Gordian knot. The swim increased my queasiness.

To lighten *Salammbo*, as well as myself, I discarded some already spoiling foodstuffs. I was disappointed, because 20 pounds of sausages were part of the deballasting. The birds following *Salammbo* immediately grabbed them and did not show any signs of being disappointed.

The weather improved on December 31, and I tried to spruce up myself and the boat. Before the old-year wash-up, as I always do when venturing into dangerous waters, I shaved my head. The farewell to the old year only increased my tension. I imagined the New Year's Eve celebration at home, and to allay my nervousness I yelled out the names of Zsuzsa and Piroska from where I stood on the deck.

I dined on Aunt Ella's fried chicken while I waited for the 24th hour. At midnight I switched on the tape player and listened to the Hungarian National Anthem. I went to the cockpit and opened the Australian champagne I had been given. Maybe it popped, but I couldn't hear it over the thundering waves. I gulped it down and sprinkled some on the deck to celebrate the occasion in style with *Salammbo*. 1991... What would its first half bring? Would I see the second half?

THE FURIOUS FIFTIES

Salammbo was not able to enjoy the champagne bath for long. The gales of the following days drenched the boat in saltwater, and troubles started immediately.

The wind indicator—changed after the capsize—was now broken once more by a wave, even though I was only at the latitude of 36° S. The Sat. Nav., repaired in Fremantle, did not last a week. I took out the sextant; I couldn't fret anymore about the failure of my electronic instruments. The jibe brake I bought in Australia worked well, and the repaired and reinforced sails worked better than when new.

Navigation was made easier by the pocket computer I had bought in Australia. It replaced the big, inconvenient tables and lengthy longhand calculations. I could calculate the average of several sights, and the fixes became more accurate. My biggest joy was *Salammbo*'s performance. The overloaded boat covered 130-140 n. miles daily.

On January 5, 6, and 7, the wind moderated to Force 4-5 and the waves abated. The temperature was 16° C (61° F), but my food spoiled surprisingly fast. Ten pounds of lemons, dough, and bacon went the way of the sausage. I also said farewell to the 20-pound pumpkin from my friend John. It had nothing wrong with it, but cooking it would have used too much energy. I had to be careful with the propane.

I rounded Cape Leeuwin, the second of the five most feared capes, a few hundred miles off the southwest corner of Australia. In honor of the occasion I cooked a festive dinner. Pasta in crab sauce with ketchup and

Parmesan cheese. Lasagna, wine, bagels, and apples.

As we left 39° South Latitude and 125° East Longitude behind, the weather stayed pleasant and sunny. I was able to sail with full sails, a rare gift on the Indian Ocean. It looked like the Forties didn't roar all the time. I heard of Nandi Fa's position: 52°13'S and 118°29'E. I expected that he would reach and pass me. After fighting his way back to South Africa with a broken rudder, Nandi had started from Port Elizabeth for Sydney. He would go north of Tasmania through the Bass Strait, but I rounded Tasmania from the south, around the South East Cape. We talked for an hour with telephone quality sound. It lifted my spirits.

This occasion prompted me to open a coconut, and I wanted to capture my magnificent opening technique on video. The cracking and the taping were perfect... the coconut was rotten. I opened one after another, but when I got similar results I dumped the whole lot out of *Salammbo*.

The next radio contact brought bad news. Zsolt Pal told me very tactfully that my wife had been involved in an accident with her car. Before I dropped the microphone, he added in a hurry that Zsuzsa was not hurt. I finished the conversation thanking God.

EXCERPTS FROM THE LOG
January 8-14, 1991

In the next few days, the weather quickly corrected itself and behaved according to the location. I kept the daily 140 n. mile average despite the northeast Force 7 wind. During the nights, phosphorescent jellyfish—like neon tubes—swam around and made me feel the run of *Salammbo*. One morning I discovered to my surprise that the deck and sail were full of soot. I was already 500 miles from the shore, but the products of a bushfire somewhere in Southern Australia were still able to blacken the boat.

The 10th of January was a black day in another way. My radio friends gave bad news. Zsuzsa, a highly qualified physical education teacher, had lost her job. I thought to myself, "What ties me to a country like that, apart from my family?"

Some new radio contacts cheered me up. Talking to Nandi Fa, I learned that his position was 45°20'S and 135°45'E. *Salammbo* and *Alba Regia* were the closest they had been to each other since Gibraltar, at just 200 miles apart. The other thing that cheered me up in this cloudy/rainy weather was the swimming news. Australian radio commented enthusiastically on the Hungarian successes at the swimming and water polo championships in Perth.

January 15-21, 1991

The Force 9 gale would not leave me alone. The rainclouds and showers did not permit any success with a sun sight for 38 hours; my sextant and I succeeded only in getting repeatedly drenched. When I finally got a fix—45°33'S and 140°10'E—it was evident that I had passed the South East Cape, the southernmost point of Tasmania. I was now on the third and biggest ocean of my voyage... it carried the misnomer of the Pacific Ocean. The temperature was 10° C (50° F), so I didn't have to cool the can of beer I drank to celebrate reaching the new ocean.

Talking to Nandi on the 16th, at 0647 hours UTC, I learned that he would arrive in Sydney in six hours. One less happy piece of news about the BOC was that one of their boats had collided with a fishing boat.

The temperature dropped to 7° C (45° F). I was feeling colder during the nights. The Pacific Ocean tried to show me its many faces. In the pouring rain the SW wind escalated from 7 to 9, and I was soaked daily. Everything was wet and damp in the cabin. The Pacific provided a varied selection of its waves. The 25- to 30-foot swells were 800-900 feet apart and rolled by very rapidly.

At 46° S and 151° E I said goodbye to the Australian ham clubs; it was the limit of their effective range. I thanked them for their help, and I was deeply touched by how carefully they transferred me to the listening ears of the New Zealanders.

I heard radio broadcasts that the combat campaign of Operation Desert Storm had begun against Iraq. On the Southern Ocean I felt very far from everything that was happening in other parts of the world, but this news upset me. Fighting the forces of nature can be desperate, but it is always honest. I think that man's fight against man is more cruel and unreasonable.

January 22-25, 1991

The weather played a joke on me. The sun came out and neither wind nor boat moved. I was virtually pegged down 200 miles from New Zealand. The only advantage was that I could take perfect fixes. I could measure the sun, the moon, and the stars. On the ceaselessly mad Indian Ocean that had been impossible.

Then the rain started, and the wind was not far behind. I couldn't complain. I heard on the radio that Sydney had been hit by the most severe hail- and rainstorm in the last 200 years. It had caused terrible destruction. Buildings were damaged, trees were felled by the hundreds, and the military had been called in to clean up the mess.

I was in a Force 4 wind 60 miles from the Snares Islands, south of New Zealand. Cape Horn was 4,701 miles from here. I reset my time, +11 Hours from Greenwich (UT). I talked daily with Istvan Pal in Sydney and regularly signed in with the New Zealand net. They were very helpful, and their weather predictions were accurate.

I became so used to the solitude that, as I was climbing into the cockpit on the 24th of January, I nearly fell back when I saw a ship. The roughly

4000-ton fishing vessel was approaching me at about 6-7 knots, and the distance was diminishing fast. I started to call the ship on the radio, and the officer on duty answered immediately. It turned out that the ship was from South Korea. They gave me their position, which coincided with my calculated one. This accuracy on my part filled me with pride. In my ebullient mood I started a conversation. Answering their questions, I explained *Salammbo*'s voyage and then started on politics. I expressed my happiness that our countries had reestablished diplomatic relations, then wished them bon voyage.

I started to cook in the cabin. After half an hour I came out to throw away the potato peelings and saw with dismay that the South Korean boat had passed me and was turning in front of me. Not understanding the maneuver, I hurriedly loaded the flare gun. Upon spying on their deck with my binoculars I immediately put the blunderbuss away. I saw that a few fishermen had blown up plastic bags with compressed air, and put their balloons in the water on long strings. The ship still crossed my path and was getting frighteningly close. It was evident that they knew their business, but I was no longer accustomed to being in the vicinity of large ships.

I didn't have to change my course an inch. I only had to reach out with the boat hook to fish the gift packages out. *Salammbo* was running fast with the following wind and, unaccustomed to such maneuvers, I accidentally put the end of the boat hook between the blades of the wind generator. One blade fell into the water and I fell into desperation. If I was left in the middle of the Pacific Ocean without energy it would be no laughing matter. Instead of fishing for presents I checked the wind generator. To my relief only two blades were broken, and I had exactly two spares.

After that I happily pulled in the bags, which contained more than just air. The gift of the South Koreans: apples, grapes, oranges, and tomatoes. I had been underway for a month, and the only vegetables I had were potatoes, onions, and garlic. I went to the radio and thanked them for the package. While I nibbled on the grapes I thought about what had happened. I had thought they would send fish, of which they must have plenty, but instead they sent things they would not be able to obtain again for months. And what you have the least of is the most precious. I was deeply touched by their selfless gesture. These are the times when the love of life and mankind glows within me.

Soon it became evident that my generous benefactor was being followed by a long convoy. I lost count trying to get a tally of them all. I warned the BOC racers by radio of their presence. I recognized that over 50 South Korean fishing boats were now plying the ocean with us.

January 26-30, 1991
I rounded the fourth cape, the southwest corner of Stewart Island. This was

the first I had passed in pleasant weather, and I was sorry that I hadn't seen any of them, since I had rounded all of them from a great distance. I resolved that I would do everything I could to ensure that the last— Cape Horn—would be an exception, regardless of the risks.

I came across seals more often, and observed that when the sun was shining they floated on the surface and slept. When waves slapped their front fins together they looked like they were praying. At other times bottlenose dolphins cavorted in *Salammbo*'s wake. One day the blow of two whales called me on deck, but the usual happened: when I got back with my camera they had already dived with a loud splash of their tails.

My position on the 29th of January was 48°54'S and 179°51'E. The west wind was Force 4, waves were moderate, the temperature was 10° C (50° F), and the humidity was 70%. I had started from Perth exactly a month ago, and today I crossed the International Date Line. I had the pleasure of experiencing the 29th of January twice.

To avoid gaining a day, I reset my watch. It was simple going east; I gained one hour for every 15 degrees locally. My navigational calculations didn't change, because I used universal time. Yet I didn't know what to do with the log.

Listening to the broadcast station brought the dangerous desire for an outing on land. The New Zealand radio broadcast lovely musical programs, and it attracted me like a magnet to that beautiful land. The reception was good on shortwave too. Shortwave gave me a great surprise on January 30. I had been discussing the daily events with the coordinator of the New Zealand net, when I noticed a familiar voice and call sign. My friend Werner was calling me! The Danish physician I had first met in Gibraltar was anchored in the yacht harbor of Sydney, close to *Alba Regia*. He had learned my frequency and times from Toni Szipola, who worked on Nandi's boat. Werner talked happily and then gave the microphone to his wife Inge. They told me that they had been constantly trying to find me on the air. Werner planned to go to Melbourne to take part in the race to Japan.

I also heard an unfortunate story from them. A couple who were friends of theirs had sailed around Africa to go to Australia and participate in the same race. After leaving Cape Town they had gotten into a great storm, and their boat capsized three times. They had to abandon the sinking yacht and get in the life raft. They were lucky their S.O.S. was heard and a helicopter from the mainland rescued them. Werner promised that he would visit me in Hungary. He said that he would definitely go, and he hoped to find me there too.

January 31 – February 2, 1991

There was other bad news over the radio. The New Zealand net had been looking for the singlehanded 31-foot sailboat *Harmonica* for days without results. The unfortunate sailor had disappeared north of my boat. The next bad news from home was for me. Zsuzsa was in the hospital. That day, the 31st, was our 16th wedding anniversary. Maybe my fellow sailor in Perth, the French Michel, had been right; he banned radios from his boat. After the home connection, I tuned into the BBC, and—right on cue—they broadcast the Ave Maria. The choir sang just like at our wedding in St. Stephen's Basilica.

The ocean showed off its strength with Force 10 winds gusting to 11. In the downpours I avoided running straight downwind, sailing on broad reaches instead. Even so I was still swamped often. The cockpit was like a bathtub after such a dousing, but with neither the bathroom's nor the water's temperature to my liking. If only I could have warmed the water that was in my boots, at the very least. The waves got into the cabin, despite the closed companionway, and my bunk was drenched. I consoled myself that at least the bunk was not tempting me in that condition. The westerly storms were followed by bright lightning, making the night even more terrifying. At the wheel I could see first the deck disappearing in the foamy waters, and then the bow cutting into and dipping in the water, the flashes were so frequent. It was better to be under cover of darkness. Why the hell should I have to watch these ugly storms at night?

It was strange—I didn't know how or why, but I could smell fire. I would never solve the puzzle, just as I would never find out from where palm fronds, mangroves, and other tropical vegetation came floating on the tops of the waves.

In the first two days of February I only went into the cabin for food and radio. Both sustained me. The coordinators of the New Zealand observation circuit, Les and Tony, worked day and night, even on weekends and holidays. They collected and transmitted all information in their sector most professionally. It was fantastic that they did it for no reward, just for their dedication to help. Their quiet, patient words were like a safety net for the helpless to hang onto.

My position on February 2: 50°01'S and 168°13'W. I crossed into the Furious Fifties. The latitude did not belie its reputation; the wind increased and the waves got higher. Where was the upper limit? On the day of the crossing I lost my nerve; I was going mad. I dropped the can of silicone spray while servicing a winch and the whole contents of the can went into the cabin. I was skating on the silicone, as well as rice that had escaped from its container. I needed a fixed point on which to hang spiritually. I put Mussorgsky and Wagner on the tape player and turned the volume to maximum.

February 3-10, 1991

On the 3rd of February at 0300 hours, the galley transposed itself to the chart table—not only the pots, but the food as well. Milk powder got into my sleeping bag. Its edibility was certainly not enhanced by mixing it with the water already in the bag. The mast hit the water with such speed that even the most securely fixed objects took off. The wild weather had one advantage: I sailed 164 n. miles in one day. *Salammbo* was now 3,150 n. miles away from Cape Horn. I figured that I could be there in a month.

The next day, at 0100 hours, the radar detector started its racket. The visibility was unusually good in the clear moonlight, but I still could not see a thing. I was uneasy, and thought to myself that only a submarine could have disappeared so fast. During the day, in the moderate Force 5 winds, I prepared for a new storm. I oiled the winches and retightened the stays. According to Les' prediction, a new 50-knot northwest wind was to be expected. The prediction came true the next day. I was between a high and a low pressure front. It rained, the temperature was 8° C (46° F), and the humidity was 80%. In the following days there was no food or sleep, but at least I was not alone. With a white flash, dolphins danced around until daybreak, and then disappeared. I couldn't learn their virtuoso movements, but I could imitate being awake all night.

Surprisingly, the water became milder on the 8th of February. The temperature went up to 10° C (50° F), and since the wind had reduced I did my deck work in a T-shirt and underwear.

At 51° South Latitude! On the radio Zsolt Pal listened in disbelief, even as he chided me for not giving tall tales about icebergs and storms.

The next day I reassured him that I was cold again. It was not so much from the outside temperature, but from developing cold shakes. Something was trying to get me—a toothache. But my stomach problems had disappeared. I had a theory that there were fewer preservatives in Australian canned foods than in the Hungarian ones. As if to prove the point, I had to throw out more spoiled cans than before. The packet soups were excellent; they tasted good and were easy to prepare—just add hot water. One of my favorites was onion soup with cheese and croutons, all in one bag. The canned meats were all the same consistency. The Dutch brown long life bread was inedible. My priority was to cook the meals fast, hoping that my small bottles of propane would last.

On February 9 and 10, on the invariably stormy seas, the speedometer often showed 10 knots. My daily performance was usually over 150 n. miles. Where would I have been with an autopilot, without the zig-zagging? The rain poured down, but the light of the cabin oil lamp was cozy. When I had a quiet hour I read Attenborough by its light, and that warmed me.

February 11-17, 1991
It was 6° C (43° F) in the cabin. Outside, the salty, damp wind cut to my bones. My fingers were numb in seconds. The specialty of these gales was

Above: *Another visitor comes by for a short stopover. All forms of life are welcome guests during such a long and lonely voyage!*

the waves. When the crest fell from the house-sized waves, the area of white foam was as big as a tennis court. The patrol flights of the birds among the waves were as difficult to explain as my own actions in that maelstrom.

Les, of the New Zealand net, warned me of a strong swell coming from the southwest. My calculated position on the 11th of February was 50°53'S and 137°44'W. I should have been maintaining a 92° heading, but because of the predicted gigantic swells I could not keep it. The waves were over 60 feet high and the breaking, falling, spraying crests changed the ocean into a white field of spume.

In the following days the rain turned to sleet and snow. I was really angry about the so-called "waterproof" heavy weather suits. They were such in name only. Zsuzsa gave one to me for Christmas—a slightly used Australian Gore-Tex suit. It seemed to be comfortable, and I could put several layers under it. It was nice, and was said to be waterproof. Yet I was soaked to my skin in this one, as I had been with the others.

For the day's chore, I sewed the batten pockets. While searching for the sewing kit, I discovered that everything on the shelves of the closed compartments was moldy and rotting. It refuted my theory that fungi needed darkness, dampness, and warmth to propagate; warmth wasn't a necessity after all.

I could not shed my ailment. During the first leg of the voyage I had never dreamt. Since leaving Australia, even during five-minute naps, I had been having muddled dreams. Sometimes I was even awakened by my own

Above: *The helm after snowfall.*

Above: *Those of us who live in the Northern Hemisphere tend to equate "southern" with "warmth"—not the case in the South Pacific! It's freezing cold, but at least there are no bugs.*

voice. Whenever I could find the time, I read Kenneth Clark's *Civilisation: A Personal View*.[46] It always calmed me down.

The animal kingdom substituted for society in that part of the world. One day a small seal nearly jumped into the cockpit, close to the wind vane. In *Salammbo*'s wake, it entertained me by playing and dancing. I opened a few cans of meat to prepare its lunch. Unfortunately, I lost my balance, and one of the cans fell into the water. I hoped that my clumsiness would not result in it wounding its mouth.

I met a new kind of bird. It looked like a marten, but could hardly fly. When *Salammbo* got close, it dived, and I couldn't see it again for several minutes. Nature's variety is so amazing that in the path of icy storms, thousands of miles from land, such a small clumsy bird somehow survives, and probably even thrives too. I don't know whether it was from seeing these birds, but the next time I read, instead of Clark and Attenborough, I turned to Micimackó (Winnie the Pooh).

On the 17th of February I crossed the 55° S Latitude. This was inside the ice limit, though according to the New Zealand radio messages it was clear up to 60° S. Les, of the New Zealand net, said goodbye to me and gave me the frequencies of the radio station in Chile. The parting increased my loneliness. Les had been more than just a voice. He was a helpful friend and a daily companion, like the hams of the Equator station. I consoled myself with the thought that new voices and new friendships would be born in the air.

February 18-21, 1991

On the 18th it rained all day, and since the wind was not stronger than Force 5, I spent a couple of hours in the closed cabin. I was still in a bad mood. I tried to help it by paging through my books. Durer's etchings took my attention for a while, and then I read the Bible. The only significant event in the day was that, after a long while, I could finally raise the broadcast of Szulofoldem ("Fatherland"), on 15160 kHz.

The next day I was successful in shooting the sun. If I could keep the 140-150 n. mile pace, I would be at Cape Horn in two weeks. The position fix had a greater significance now. *Alba Regia*, which had started with the BOC fleet from Sydney, was at 63°95'S and 129°26'W. She was closing fast, and would probably catch me. We checked each other's positions carefully during the radio contacts. Could we meet? While I was calculating *Salammbo*'s speed, it became calm. The sea was quieter and the current was significant, adding 10-20 miles daily to *Salammbo*'s run.

The calm, which was very rare in that area, gave me a splendid chance to

---

[46] Note the British spelling of "Civilisation" is intentional in this case.

wash and shave. In the clear skies I could measure 5 stars in addition to the sun and moon.

The following two days chased away the memory of those quiet hours. In the northeast Force 8 gale, the gusts tore off the block of the third reefing line on the mainsail, making my mood even worse. On the 21st of February I escaped the pouring rain by getting into the cabin just in time to hear the BBC's announcement about John Martin's accident. While racing in the BOC, he had hit an iceberg. One of the other racers rescued him from his sinking boat. I resolved that, if possible, I would pay more attention to the ice information broadcast.

February 22, 1991
Gales with large swells. In the cabin the thermometer showed 3° C (37° F), but since the thermometer could measure no lower, it was probably colder. The barometer fell to 95 kPa, and since that was also the bottom value of that instrument, I wondered what would happen if the air pressure in fact fell lower. Fighting the wheel, my fingers froze. I was drenched in cold sweat. I wrote in my log: "It can only be worse in the lime pit."

In the hours of the night, I crossed the 60° S Latitude. The radio station of the BOC fleet announced that there were five boats in this crazy region: two French racers, an Australian, Nandi Fa with the *Alba Regia*, and me, the non-racer with *Salammbo*. According to the bulletins one BOC racer sighted an iceberg on the 57° S Latitude, but they said that there was no danger in our area for the time being. I kept in contact with Nandi on the radio at every possible moment. His present position was 61°34' S and 114°37' W. He told me that in the 70- to 80-knot winds, while stopped and with no sails on, his boat had lain flat on the water despite the ballast. Regardless of the wild surroundings, we excitedly discussed the possibility of us meeting. Zsolt Pal butted in from the Equator station: Was I going to the left, out of the storm? I told him I was in it, but not in its center.

February 23, 1991
Position: 60°20'S and 108°00'W. Heading: 60°. Wind: Force 6.
My video recorder was a smart contraption. It indicated that it was not going to work because of the high humidity.

Nandi and I adjusted our positions during our conversations. We worked out the right tactics for our meeting. The storm spared no one. Several boats were knocked down. The prognosis was not encouraging. A Force 10 storm was to be expected.

ALBA REGIA IN SIGHT
I entered in the log for the 24th that I hoped the day would bring an extraordinary event. Since dawn the only extraordinary thing had been the

cold. It was around the freezing point, and snow was falling. According to the BBC, since John Martin's accident the race in this ocean was not for the trophy, but for survival. I listened to the radio conversations of the participants. Those sharing the dangers carefully watched each other's progress. The racers in the area of the 60s were bunched in one group, and I could feel their concern for each other from their conversations. The BBC was right—it was about survival now; the race could continue on the Atlantic under more normal circumstances.

Since I had started listening to these conversations, I didn't feel alone. Remembering my solitude on the Indian Ocean, I felt like a few boats in the area of the 60s made the ocean crowded.

I talked to Nandi all the time on the radio. There was no wind or snow that could prevent our rendezvous. I was so excited that I felt like running up and down the boat. The suspense was transmitted on the airwaves between *Salammbo* and *Alba Regia*. Nandi gave his coordinates regularly; his satellite navigator updated his position every 15-20 minutes. My own position was 59°31'S and 102°42'W. We modified our respective courses so that we would meet during daylight.

I ran to the radio from the wheel. "We are within ten miles of each other, you must see me on the radar!" I shouted into the set. Not waiting for an answer, I ran back to the deck following my instincts. I looked around and my heartbeat raced. On the horizon I saw the sails of *Alba Regia*.

It was fantastic! I jumped back into the cabin and shouted into the microphone, "I see you!" In the minutes that followed I switched between the radio and the wheel. I tried to keep to the south to cross his path, because as I saw it the *Alba Regia* kept her course. At the next exchange Nandi asked whether I was sure it was him that I saw, because he hadn't seen anything. Back on deck. I fired a green flare from the gun, then watched through binoculars as *Alba Regia* moved. Nandi was turning towards *Salammbo*.

Still out of hearing distance, but shouting and dancing, we greeted each other. *Alba Regia* was getting closer meter by meter, and Nandi started to circle *Salammbo*. Cameras and video cameras were busy on both sides, and the photo session was sometimes interrupted by Indian war cries of excitement. *Alba Regia* came closer to *Salammbo*, and I soon found out the reason for Nandi's daring maneuver. The bag thrown from his boat fell into the water, and when I fished it out I found out how lucky I was to have the bag land in the water rather than on deck. Inside were a small bottle of Johnny Walker whisky, relatively fresh biscuits, oranges, and chocolate. Out of the bag I also pulled Nandi's greetings.

It was difficult to get away from the site and our feelings. The sun was setting; night was coming soon. The feeling weighed on me that I had to be

Above: *An historic moment for Hungarian Sporting:*
My rendezvous with Nandor Fa in the Pacific Ocean.

Above: *Nandi and I captured the moment and exchanged*
the photos afterwards. Here you can feel my excitement.

Above: *Nandi and I circled one another, getting as many photos as we could, neither one of us wanting this wonderful meeting to end.*

Above: *It was thrilling not only to be a part of such a milestone for Hungarian sports, but also to punctuate the constant solitude with the company of a friend. How many people ever have the chance to meet up with an old friend in the middle of the Pacific Ocean?*

alone again. I urged Nandi on; he was in a race in which every second and mile counted. We exchanged a "goodbye," and the much bigger *Alba Regia* left *Salammbo* behind.

We continued to discuss it on the radio, time and again. In the evening the meeting was the main theme of discussion on the international radio circles. In addition to Equator and a few other Hungarian radio hams, other hams joined in from Sydney, Montevideo, Sao Paulo, New Zealand, and the United States. Gyuri, from Montevideo, commented at length on the event, and everybody agreed that the meeting of two Hungarian sailors on the South Pacific was really a milestone in Hungarian sporting history.

That evening was wonderful. We chatted away our tensions and fears. Everything looked beautiful that night. Nandi expressed it most concisely: The world was wonderful, people were wonderful. We were charged up, but it was necessary; extraordinary days were ahead of us.

After the radio session I stuffed myself with the fruits, and I enjoyed Nandi's other gift, the biscuits (actually a very special Hungarian biscuit called Pogacsa, baked by Hungarian immigrants in Sydney). I packed away the whisky and the message and went back to the wheel.

9

CAPE HORN
(1991 February 25 — March 5)

"Illi robur et aes triplex circa pectus erat, qui fragilem truci commisit pelago ratem prinus."
("There was oak and a triple layer of bronze around the heart of the man who first launched a fragile craft on the savage open sea.")
—Horace, Odes 1.3

I WANTED, IN SOME WAY, TO STORE AND PRESERVE THE effect of the momentous rendezvous of the 24th and those invigorating happy hours on the radio. I was aware by that time of how much my nerves, feelings, and moods could affect my circumstances, for better or worse. In this situation, I was energized by every new event and happy moment. A few days away from Cape Horn, to prepare to cross those most highly feared waters, I wanted to shape my person into good order. It would not be possible to proceed with my physical condition the way it was after the exhausting two-month voyage I had just endured.

The weather did not help, for in the following three days it became colder. Snow flurries swept the deck, although from time to time the sun came out. But in the cold the snow stayed on the deck for 3-4 hours. In the snow-weakened wind I sailed with full plan, but the tempo dictated by the Force 3-4 southwest wind left me unsatisfied. I felt it would be better to pass quickly through what was inevitable.

The unsteady wind also held back the BOC fleet. On the 26th of February, I took refuge in the cabin from a new snow squall as I radioed

Jose, the skipper of the Spanish racer. This oldest racer, at 62 years of age, had protested angrily before that Nandi and I had occupied the frequency for hours. This time we made friends with one another, inviting each other for a visit at home. We figured that we were the only two left in the area of 59° S Latitude.

The leading boats of the race should reach Punta Del Este in Uruguay in 10-12 days. They calculated that the first racer would round Cape Horn on the 28th. Thinking of my more Spartan boat with its defective instruments, I was consoled to hear how the other captains cursed the products of some big name manufacturers. Their complaints revealed that they had many problems with Lewmar blocks and hatches.

The wind was still below Force 3 in the west-southwest breeze. I kept to the 90° easterly course. But on the 27th the snow slowly changed to rain. I had time to fill the diesel tank of the motor, then climbed the mast to fix a loose bracket of the radar reflector. After the climbing performance I realized that my fitness level was terrible.

EXCERPTS FROM THE LOG

February 28, 1991

Since 3:00 in the morning, ice and snow had beaten on the deck. This heavenly "blessing" came in short cloudbursts, which brought stiffer winds. The previous night a dense black cloud mass had appeared in the sky, just like the ones that warn the sailors on the north coast of Lake Balaton of an approaching storm. Expecting the same, I had left only the storm sails on, but the storm did not arrive. I was too tired to put the main on in the hope of achieving greater speed, preferring to sleep instead. It turned out to be a wise decision, for the wind changed gear to 50-60 knots, and the boat started to run wild.

I heard on the radio that the Chilean Coast Guard was looking for John Martin, who had been rescued by his fellow racer. The unlucky BOC racer would get to port in a patrol boat, rather than in his own craft.

I was constantly studying myself—not my appearance, but my psyche. I was able to say that there were no abnormal symptoms, no unusual habits or actions. I had no hallucinations or visions. The only thing I did discover was my frequent discussion with animals. For example, an albatross landed on *Salammbo*'s wake one day, 5-10 meters from the boat. I started speaking to it, and when it got out of hearing range it flew closer once again. This was repeated several times. I opened a can of fish for it, but it showed no interest, fell behind, and then flew back once again. It was evident that it did not need food, just a few warm words.

March 1, 1991

The day's event: "Today is the 14th birthday of my daughter Piroska." The weather did not care about the celebration; big rainclouds were coming, the wind got up to Force 6, and the barometer fell steadily from 98.9 kPa. My position was 58°04'S and 086°30'W. I thanked the sun for showing itself, if only for a short time, allowing for the fix.

I was not the only one occupied by the antics of the animals. On that day, Jose Ugarte and an Australian racer had a long discussion on the radio about albatrosses. Jose dug up a bird book from his boat's library and read part of it on the radio. I was surprised when I heard about the extraordinary habits of these birds. Albatrosses can fly 1-2 thousand nautical miles without eating anything. To do this without hurting themselves, they must have perfectly insulating plumage and a very energy-efficient flight. The wonders of nature are limitless...

After the lecture I took a look in the sextant's mirror and found that I looked much worse than an albatross. I had pimples on my face; I didn't know where from. It was not new that my fingers were swollen from the frost, but my fingernails had also started to crack and bleed. At the last sail change my fingers had drawn long red lines on the sails.

Going back to the cabin, I heard a radio warning for the BOC racers: "An Australian container ship is nearing Cape Horn, look out for it!" Jose came in with bad news again: a 46-foot sailboat sailing from Hawaii to the Falkland Islands had disappeared. After such news, there were always a couple of minutes of silence on the air. We all thought about the unknown fellow sailor.

March 2, 1991

At the morning radio session, Zsuzsa was at the Equator station, with Zsolt interpreting. We told each other what we could, and that was not much. Radio traffic has strict rules; the frequencies are not for family matters, and don't allow any intimacy. It would have been nice to have a telephone conversation to discuss in detail what was happening at home, or to say something about our feelings, before I faced the hard days to come. According to my plans, the next telephone booth would be three months away in Gibraltar.

The wind was weak. It was maddening to crawl so slowly towards Cape Horn. The barometer fell quickly to 97.4 kPa. According to my calculation of the moon's position, it looked like I would be in a full moon storm... the last thing I wanted.

March 3, 1991

It was completely overcast and raining hard, making it impossible to get a fix. My estimated position went into the log: 56°23'S and 073°03'W. I felt I should be around that place. There were birds other than albatrosses around the boat; they could have come from the South American continent or the islands.

It was another big day. I allowed an extra portion of water for my bath and hair wash and shave—4 liters instead of 2. I prepared myself for Cape Horn like a groom for his wedding. Other similarities came to my mind— someone readied for his funeral is also spruced up on the outside. Away with those thoughts; I got out the chart again.

It would have been nice to get in closer and see something, but the risk was too great. Many islands and rocks were in the way. So much the worse that I had only an estimated position for the boat, but that could not be helped. Once again I checked the stowed equipment, which might move or come away in the heavy seas. Once I finished the log, that would be stashed away too. There was no certainty that I would have time for such peaceful entries in the coming days. If we could make contact, the hams at the Equator station would tape our conversation.

EXCERPT FROM THE LOG OF THE
EQUATOR AMATEUR RADIO STATION

Szekesfehervar (HA4EHQ – Equator Headquarters) from Salammbo at Cape Horn. Azimuth 82°.
1991. 03. 06 Wednesday. 1230 UTC, signed on 21278 MHZ 44LP (taped)
"—HA4EHQ, HG5S/MM Calling, Zsolt, Karcsi, thanks for the confirmation. Roger. My reception is hundred percent as well. I am happy that we could connect despite the wild goings-on the day before yesterday. I could give a few fragments, only a few sentences about what happened. I wasn't always on the frequency, I had to monitor 4143.6 MHZ and VHF channel 16 in case a ship comes this way or something requires quick communication. I will, well, I try to summarize the two and a half days. It will be difficult, don't get mad if I talk so excited, but it was terrible, a veritable nightmare. Also a frantic adventure and thanks to God, a great happiness. I couldn't explain it better later at home, it cannot be really explained, it must be seen, be experienced. I couldn't wish for my worst enemy to live through something like this. I couldn't wish something so bad to anybody. Back to you, Zsolt, how do you read me?

—HA4EHQ, HG5S/MM, Roger, I continue. The madness started two and a half days ago, that is, rounding the Cape lasted nearly three days. I count the rounding from the moment when the visibility was reduced to 400-500 feet, that is when you see only as far as your nose. I was being aggravated all the time. Firstly, it was the visibility. Through the two and a half days it rained cats and dogs, with snow, sometimes ice. It didn't help the visibility, but it kept me awake. The weather prevented celestial observations and coastal plotting. I had no way to fix my position. For that reason—wait a little, how much?—at least for seventy hours I did not sleep a wink. I didn't dare to fall asleep, or even to sit down. I was afraid that I would fall asleep, so most of the time, I was out on the deck. The first day it was a 50- to 60-knot west wind with 65-knot gusts, with the sea going with it on the top of the swells. Average wave height could be 40 feet, but a well-grown one broke right behind *Salammbo*, and the boat fell nearly vertically nose down into the trough, and for a second it seemed that it would pitchpole. The wave accelerated inexplicably to 35-40 knots and the boat, cutting the wave to the height of the pulpit, started to surf. At the same time I nearly drowned, because the breaking crest kept swamping the wheel, raising the water level to my mouth.

I was really lucky. Later, with higher waves, it would have produced a full pitchpole. I didn't know then, that it was only a foreplay, the Cape Horn waves were only building up. On top of it the next day, the wind turned to east-southeast, and it can be imagined—if it can be imagined—what kind of seas were produced by the interference with the new waves caused by the contrary winds. The wind contrary to the current produced terribly confused seas. After the wind shift, I had to tack, which made my position estimate more difficult. For the next day, this E-SE wind increased to 50-55 knots, and the rain never stopped.

I could have decided not to give a damn for it and give up the adventure to actually see it, since I was safely below it, I could have rounded it around the 57th parallel, far from the islands and all that mess. But that would be something like climbing Mount Everest and turning back 500 feet below the peak. So I committed the foolishness. I wanted to see the Cape at all costs, and that was what I nearly paid. That's why I got close to islands and hazards. With that poor visibility and no accurate fix, it is upsetting.

I have to say, that it is difficult to distinguish between storm and storm. Each has its character, which shows in the waves, currents, wind strength, its steadiness or lack of it. But say on the Indian Ocean, where I had fine gales and storms, it does not matter if you are 50 miles away, it gives you a chance to avoid the storm center, and you can apply proper avoidance techniques. There is plenty of space, no shore, or rocks, and you can maneuver comfortably. Down on the 60° Latitude, where I met Nandi, I could—with difficulty—shoot the sun, but here it was no use to have a full moon, I couldn't see the bow, especially when the dense sleet came down. I had to tack, you know, into the 50- to 60-knot winds and I had only a vague idea that I was around the Ramirez Islands.

HA4EHQ, Roger, I didn't mention it, though it was very disturbing; the ship traffic. I found out from the radio traffic that there are whales around the islands, and there was somewhere a naval vessel, then comes the BOC field. I heard that the bigger ones, the 60-footers are fighting hard and the 50-footers capsize one after the other. You can imagine that this news didn't lift me up, knowing they had satellite navigators and radars to watch the shores, when I was at the wheel day and night.

The organization was good, the BOC organizers asked the *Golverino*, a ship of the Chilean Coast Guard, to be in readiness in case of trouble. It was the ship which took John Martin on, the South African chap, and this ship anchored 20 miles behind Cape Horn, in a quiet, protected cove. The racers reported to her in order, well, I thought, I can report too. I told them on the radio that I am here too. I don't quite know where, but just let them know that I am here. It is more than nothing, you understand, it is psychological, it satisfied me, though I knew they will be unable to help if anything happens.

I tell you now that I had a bad premonition about rounding Cape Horn, besides the storm and anything else. I didn't tell you before, but I give significance to the numbers. I had, so far, three very difficult birthdays, they repeated exactly every 19 years. The first, when I was born. The second when I was 19 and a seaman in the Bay of Biscay, we got into such a storm with the ship *Raba*, that the captain, who had sailed for 30 years, said that he never before saw anything like that. The ship was listing 23°, and we shoveled the shifted oil pressings [our cargo at that time] to the other side and nearly drowned in the cargo. Well, one time I'll tell you in detail. And now after 19 years, you know I will have my 38th birthday in two days, the Cape was somewhere in front of me.

My premonition of things turning bad materialized. As the storm increased and the wind turned to east-southeast. Imagine what seas will develop when an established wave system hits head on another wave-shaping wind. What interferences and wave clashings it will produce, and on top of it there is the current. The chart says that it is between 1 and 3.5 knots, but for one who cannot establish his position it doesn't matter whether it is 1 or 3.5 knots.

As I say, the situation got worse, I could run down into the cabin for minutes only, and the way it is with my luck, the propane tank ran empty. I nearly froze, I could hardly move my fingers. Changing the tanks was impossible because of the water continually dousing the cockpit. A lot of water got into the closed cabin space, and I wanted to make a cup of hot tea! As long as the wind was from the west, I was out on the deck all the time, to get rain in my face to keep me awake, to turn quickly if I see a rock or island within 150 feet.

Out of the BOC boats, I could contact only one or two on the radio, but it wasn't enough time for conversations. I talked to the skipper of the 50-foot *Spirit of Ipswich*, who was behind me and knew his own position, to call me if he picks me up on his radar. There wasn't much of a chance for that because his radar had an 18-mile range and we were probably farther than that from each other. He did not see me and I, with my bare eyes, saw absolutely nothing and nobody. Out of the 50-footers, I got in contact with an Australian fellow, the skipper of *Buttercup*, who recounted his adventures at length. He said that he never saw such a storm like that and he capsized a few times. This didn't sound encouraging, when I tried with burning eyes to penetrate the curtain of rain and snow.

Now, besides using that hang-up method for alarm-clock, I was turning my brains around like an old-fashioned calculator to figure where I may be. Instead of the kaput instruments—you know of all that—I had to feed into the computer on my neck all navigational data, wind speed, boat speed, course, current, leeway, etc., etc., so I could have a guess about the position of the boat. Then I heard during the night that the wind tore to pieces the sails of one of the French BOC racers, only the shreds were flying on the deck, so everybody had their problems in that area.

So I couldn't relax for a moment, I had to tack. The wind came from the front, and the spray dodger I had made in Australia made it possible for me to take off the top hatch. I let the boards in. I could now put my head out of the companionway and look out through the window of the dodger without climbing out on the deck. To prevent falling asleep, I hung my chin on the hatch frame, and when I dozed off, I hung myself, which woke me up in a hurry. That time I in those circumstances, worthy of Jack London, I couldn't give a hoot whether I would ever see the Cape. I wasn't interested in it, just to get out of here.

So morning came. It was the 5th of March. I guessed that I was roughly in the right area and tried to keep an easterly course. I sailed higher up to the wind to 60-70°. I estimated, that if I could keep this angle, around 5:00pm I would round the Cape. I went down into the cabin, I couldn't stand the freezing any longer, also the wind was 35-40 knots and sleet came down. And then, at noon—in fact half past eleven—the snow let up a bit, and a small opening seemed to appear between the clouds. I was praying for a little luck, to have a glimpse of the sun after two and a half days. I took the sextant and climbed on deck. As I went up there, I saw it, I saw Cape Horn in front of me—the big rock rising from the ocean.

I can't do it. It is really impossible to explain the feelings after moving blindly around in the dark, after guessing, estimating, hoping; all of a sudden the dreaded Cape Horn stands there. It was really moving, a navigational accomplishment. Out of the five dangerous Southern Capes, I have the fifth. Of those I could round only the New Zealand South East Cape in tolerable, non-stormy conditions. It was such a glorious feeling to navigate to the shores of Western Australia, then the memorable meeting with Nandi along the 60th Latitude, then the peak of it all, reaching the Horn. I felt that finding it was not only because of my surprisingly good estimations, but some unexplainable inner instinct, like the one guiding the Vikings or Polynesian navigators towards their goal into the remote parts of the world.

I have to tell you honestly, standing there on the deck, I started to cry.

At once the tension came out of me, the total exhaustion and limitless happiness. Shelving the sextant, I ran for the waterproof camera and video camera. The wind was still on and hail started, but I did not care, this had to be preserved for history, even if the ice beats up the camera. In the meantime I was steering, trying to get closer and closer to the wish and dread of all sailors, the Cape.

Above: *My first view of the great and ominous Cape Horn.*

Now, I should tell you what it looks like, but I can in no way illustrate its dramatic and poetic impact. The gray mass of rocks rising from the sea is like a classical composition with triple symmetry, something like the Laocoön Group's tragic majesty.[47] In me it evoked the symbol of the Holy Trinity, as it looks, spitting the weather over the sailors parading by the waves, and accepts, with the dignity of the Lord of Oceans, the homage of the prostrating worshippers. This is Cape Horn, beautiful and fear-evoking, the real Holy Trinity of nature, to which a painful pilgrimage leads.

During photographing it came to my mind that I should celebrate. I remembered that somewhere in the boat there was some champagne kept for this purpose, but there was just no way to find it. I had no strength for it, and the storm created such a chaos in the boat that a neglected pigsty or public lavatory would look elegant in comparison. I did so much in the cabin. I took off a floorboard, found that military quick-warmer with spirit and wick, just enough to warm up a soup. I ate it out of the can. This was

---

[47] "The Laocoön Group": a reference to the famous Greek sculpture of *Laocoön and His Sons*, which depicts the three mythical Trojan men struggling in pain as they are attacked by sea serpents.

the celebration at Cape Horn.

It would be nice to eat a full dinner once again, dry off and get out of the wet garments. I hope that on the way to the Falklands, I will find time enough for it. One more thing Zsolt, sorry that I mixed up the items, we should find a good diesel mechanic. The question is: How much can one dilute diesel with kerosene? That is, in what ratio can I add kerosene to diesel without harming the engine? My diesel is getting low; I had to use even the oil from the lamp. The stores are disappearing fast, and I have 7000 more miles to Gibraltar. Thanks for the help, boys.

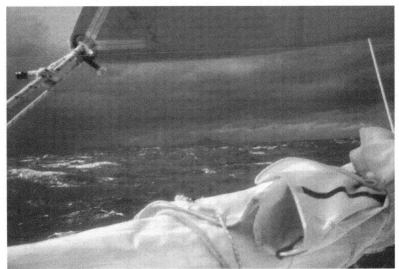

Above: *Where the childhood dream is realized: looking upon Cape Horn in the distance as storm clouds roll in.*

H4EHQ. It is HG5S/MM I have to say goodbye now. The wind is turning and there are islands close to me. Tomorrow on the usual frequency. Please give my regards to my friends, to everybody who helped. One more thing I would like to ask, please do—how should I say it—kiss Zsuzsa and Piroska for me."

10

UNDER STARRY SKIES
(1991 March 6 — April 16)

"Emancipation from the bondage of the soil is no freedom for the tree."
—Rabindranath Tagore

IN THE FOLLOWING DAYS, *SALAMMBO* QUICKLY LEFT CAPE
Horn behind with its menacing islands and rocks. The speed was the result
of 45- to 50-knot gale force winds as well as the Falkland current. I rounded
a few islands within visible distance. It was awkward that I messed up my
navigation close to the shore, mistaking the rocky mountains of Tierra Del
Fuego for the Estados Islands. Sailing on the Atlantic again, I kept the 50°
heading towards the Falklands. I planned to leave the islands about 60-80
miles to the east. I was satisfied with my progress. It took 64 days from
Fremantle to Cape Horn, which is an average of 125 n. miles a day.
Nonetheless, if I had been able to do double that figure it still would have
been too slow for me; the Atlantic was, after all, the way home.

For a while I did not care about the 7,000 miles to Gibraltar, nor was I
disturbed by the hail brought by the swirling winds. Freed from the
depressing memory of the past days and buoyed by the joy of passing Cape
Horn, I changed the sails and stood watch for long hours, reinvigorated. I
still hated the icy cold as before; I just trusted that going north quickly
would eventually make the temperature pleasant. Finally it was time to
change the gas bottle and to cook the first excellent dinner. I ate a flame-
hot chicken ragout soup and opened a can of corn.

Other than the homey corner with the range, everything else—including myself—was a disaster area. The falls, bumps, and hits I had sustained in the strong storms left my body covered with scars and blue spots. My hands were swollen, my fingernails were torn, and the bloody stripes on the sails had not yet washed away. The veins on my arms and legs were inflamed and visible from the marathon exertions. The cabin didn't show a better picture; clothing and other items had flown out of their places and were lying all over, soaked with seawater. I couldn't do anything with the bruises, just grin and bear them. But the disorder in the cabin would not let me relax, and whenever the rain or hail let up, I was busy cleaning up and drying my things. The huge swell had replenished the water inside. Water was even dripping from the knobs of the radio.

On March 8, I celebrated my 38th birthday. Reflecting on the 19-year cycles of dramatic events, I thought back 19 years to the Atlantic Ocean storm I had described to Zsolt on the radio…

* * *

DRAMATIC BIRTHDAY

Exactly 19 years earlier, we sailed on the freighter *Raba* from Turkey to Sweden with the holds full of oil pressings to be used for fodder. Our course was through the Bay of Biscay, famous for its storms. The storm that caught us could compare easily with its Southern Ocean brothers. The biggest problem was that the *Raba* (formerly known as the *Duisburg*), built in 1951 and outdated, was carrying the restrictive dictates of the peace treaties that followed World War II. To guard against the rebuilding of German industry (to be used supposedly in armament manufacturing), the shipbuilding industry was tightly regulated. One concern was that the ship could be scuttled immediately. In practice it meant that the four normally waterproof bulkheads of the *Raba* were cut through, and it was without vertical compartment walls (shifting boards) that would prevent the cargo from shifting. This dictate had caused the *Brandenburg*, *Raba*'s sister ship, to sink in exactly two minutes when it ran into a storm in the Channel.

We were reminded of *Brandenburg*'s tragedy when leaving Cape Finisterre. The northwest storm hit us with its full force. The otherwise well-built ship became increasingly airborne, spending more time in the air than in the water. It is difficult to make a 4600-ton, 350-foot-long mass of iron dance like a ballet soloist, but that was exactly what the heaving and falling fully-laden ship resembled as the waves tossed her. After two days, the hands moved from the rear quarters into midships. The waves hitting the port side of the ship were bending the stanchions and deck equipment like paper. Walking outside was dangerous even with the use of grab lines. The wooden doors of the upper structures had steel coverings, but the sea still found its way into the living quarters.

Cooking and eating became simple. Two sailors would hold the cook while he prepared the one-course meal. We wedged ourselves into various corners to spoon the food out of canteens.

We had been wallowing for a week in the Bay, which normally could be crossed in two days, when it happened. Suddenly an unusually strong wave kicked the ship with a sharp bang.

Tearing open the door, we ran out to see a surprising sight. The door of the corridor leading to the rear—two and a half inches thick—surged toward us on a cold stream of water. The Bosun was wrestling with the door to stem the tide. When the water came down the stairs leading to the upper floor, only the fish were missing to make it a true seascape. The biggest concern, though, was the new attitude of the ship. She listed to starboard and refused to right herself. Hungarians make good sailors, so instead of panicking we started to work quickly. Forming a bucket brigade, we emptied the water into the shower and the head. The extraordinary wave had even reached the machine room via the smokestack.

The crucial moment came when we tried to turn the ship away to have the wind from behind, because the heeling angle caused by the waves and the shifted cargo had reached the critical limit. Having a capsize in mind, the ship's carpenter let the lumber on the deck free so that we would have something to hang onto if we were thrown into the water. The radio operator contacted a British naval vessel not far from us.

Following the First Mate, fourteen of us clambered into the No. 1 hold carrying shovels. By the light of our flashlights we sunk into the oil pressings like Lilliputians, digging hopelessly into the mass. The Chief shoveled silently, with great determination. His solo act inspired the team. Tons of material were shoveled first into the centerline and then to the port side, countering the chance that we might drown in the pressings if there were a capsize. By morning the blisters on our hands had become blood blisters. During our brief recesses, we fell like sacks of potatoes into the dusty cargo. Late in the morning the ship finally straightened, and we came back on deck like freed galley slaves.

The British Royal Navy ship was at our heels ready for rescue, earning top marks for both seamanship and comradeship. The concern of our guardian was not without foundation; several ships had already been lost or damaged in the storm. Later we understood the Greek sailors who, according to ancient legends, superstitiously never shaved when crossing the Bay of Biscay.

* * *

Thinking back on what had happened 19 years earlier, I developed the cold shakes, even with Cape Horn behind me. I chased the bad memories away with a real birthday dinner. The dishes: Australian chicken soup with corn and toast, a slice of "temesvar" from the military supply with Italian pasta, and finally chocolate biscuits with Australian dessert wine.

The 8th of March stayed in my memory because of the experiences of the BOC racers. The Australian skipper, Don McIntyre, reported that his boat, *Buttercup*, had everything broken in the rear by the 65-knot wind. Joshua Hall, one of the English racers, told us how he had found shelter with one of the Chilean Patrol vessels. Josh had his boom broken, so instead of aiming for the Cape he went for the ship, where he was received with a hot shower and cold beer. The next morning snow covered everything. The Brit praised the beauty of the snowy peaks. The Chileans helped to mend his boom, and then he took off again. I was put off by the laxity of the BOC rules of contest. My own organizers only permitted outside help for *Salammbo* during the one stop in Australia.

EXCERPTS FROM THE LOG

The biggest event during that period was that the mercury in the thermometer started to move, and with some effort it reached +5° C (41° F). The birds were getting more colorful. There were divers as well as albatrosses. The ocean was covered with green floating vegetation. I didn't know how to account for the dead birds I saw floating on those green islands.

The wind slackened with the rain, giving me some time to spend with the radio. I did not only listen to the hams, but also to the Falkland radio programs. On the 10th of March I passed within 40 miles of the capital of the islands, Port Stanley.

During my voyage I had never had such a desire to go ashore as I did here. I have always been intrigued by small communities that break off from larger populations. They were more natural and human, which was reflected in their colorful and interesting programs. There was excitement in the air, because the Duke of Edinburgh was expected for the anniversary of the Falklands War. There was an intimacy in the life of the community. Even the passengers on the inter-island plane were announced by name on the radio, and it was interesting to listen to the details of a job announcement. Everybody knew everybody else.

March 11-15, 1991
I noted with the happiness of a fan that *Alba Regia* had reached Punta Del Este on March 11, 0913 hours. After the successful rounding of Cape Horn, the BOC field would spend Easter there before the last leg of the race to Newport, RI.

The weather was variable. Sometimes the wind stopped for a few hours and I could leave the top of the companionway hatch open. The 10° C (50°

F) air pleasantly ventilated the cabin. When I calculated that I had crossed 50° S Latitude, I celebrated with a bath and hair wash.

It was advisable to hurry with the ablutions. I felt sure that after a quiet spell, the wind would start to scream. Sure enough it got up to 60-70 knots from the northwest, which was announced by the swells. The airwaves also brought bad news. Sadly Yoko Tada, the Japanese BOC racer, had committed suicide in Sydney. When he had to give up the race, he gave up his life.

The gale turned to west-southwest. Its strength, like that of the waves, did not abate. It drove *Salammbo* to a record run of 180 n. miles in 24 hours. The horse always runs faster heading for the barn. The downside was that the ongoing rain prevented me from drying my clothes, and I craved a hot bath.

There was a colorful interruption in the gray weather when a big shark crossed the boat's path. It was about 20 feet long. At one point, about a half mile from the boat, I saw the blow of two whales, but they did not come any closer. I told Karcsi Nyemcsek that I saw a new kind of bird over the boat. In answer to his questions I tried to give an accurate description: the size of a pigeon but slimmer, color of anisette, its head reminded me of a Boeing 747. Karcsi showed signs of fantasizing, saying he could practically see the bird.

On the 15th of March (the day Hungarians celebrate the 1848 uprising against the Austrian Habsburgs), the bad weather could not prevent me from patriotically dressing the yacht. The wind nearly tore away my red-white-green flag, but I listened to the national anthem on tape in a decorated boat.

March 16-22, 1991
Position: 41°00'S and 041°04'W.
It was only three hours difference from Greenwich Mean Time (UTC). In the pleasant 10-knot westerly there were hardly any waves. The pleasure of those days was the sudden change in the weather to a warm 16° C (61° F). Finally I was able to open the closed storage spaces, and the moldy items went on deck. My personal pleasure was in changing my thermals to a T-shirt and shorts. I had not had such pleasant sailing in the last half year. There was very little heel, and it was unusual that I could stand upright—therefore I hit my head on everything.

The happiness was not without clouds; more and more things gave up the ghost. The shade glasses of the sextant fell out, and the Kevlar lines broke. As the wind weakened, the wind generator charged less and less. The solar panel, which had not been used for a while, was utterly ineffectual; one of its poles was completely corroded. Eight feet had been torn off the foot of one of the jibs. The cheek of one of the sheet blocks had broken.

Things had just become fatigued. I was to sew for days. And at night I read only by the light of the oil lamp; I had to be careful with the diesel.

On March 18 I crossed the 38th parallel. After such a long time, I was pleased to see flying fish again. There were fewer birds, but the sight of armies of dolphins made up for it. On the crest of great swells, they jumped in formation to several meters high. When they splashed down it sounded like gunfire. After the show, the troupe simply disappeared.

In the following days the spring weather vanished, and 30- to 40-knot northeast winds lashed the seas. The weather was damp and sultry. Since the 21st of March, the sun had had a northerly declination. I tried to catch it, but it was not easy. I was in the descending part of the Trades, and as the coming days would prove, the winds came from all over. On the other hand the radio brought more good news: my daughter Piroska was admitted to the high school of her choice, and my French friend, Michel, had successfully rounded Cape Horn and moored at the Falklands.

I spent those days taking inventory. First I surveyed my food stocks. The situation was not rosy; I only had 15 cans of sardines and 15 cans of meat left. There was pasta, rice, mashed potatoes, and soup enough. The 150 liters (40 gallons) of drinking water should be enough for the 2 months to Gibraltar, but I had to reduce the half pail of water I used for bathing. After the inventory I listened with envy on the radio. A program had been arranged for the Easter arrival of the BOC racers in Uruguay—everything from shows to water skiing.

March 21-31, 1991

Unusual, foreboding weather arrived. The seemingly permanent low clouds prevented celestial navigation, and the strong southwest swells sprayed water in their fast gallop to *Salammbo*'s sails. On some nights the moon hid. There was a mysterious fog, and it was very chilly. I felt depressed because I could not see any living creatures, not even birds. The south-southwest wind made me think that I was already in the area of the Trades, until the wind started to come from across the front.

According to the estimated position I was around 29° S and 031° W. I was still satisfied with *Salammbo*'s progress. On March 31, for example, I covered 131 n. miles. I felt the need for some activity, so I shaved my head bald. I didn't miss freshwater showers; it was enough to just go on deck during the frequent rain showers. Choosing food became easier: just one dish daily… rice with peas.

On March 26, 36- to 40-knot gusts made me jump, and it was so warm that even my watch strap was burning me. True! That was the only thing I was wearing. The plant I bought in Calgary had survived everything so far. Unlike me, it loved the heat, and it started thriving again. During the days I cooled myself with seawater; at night I cooked in my own juice. Therefore on the 28th I decided on a revolutionary step: I would spend my nights in the cockpit. From my sleeping bag I viewed the beautiful sky, with full moon and loaded with stars. Right overhead was Sirius; in the morning it was Antares of the Scorpion.

There was nothing enjoyable on the boat at that time except the view of the night sky. In the dying wind the boat slowed down, and I had time to finish sewing the torn sails.

On the second to last day of March, I had an unpleasant surprise. I removed a floorboard while searching for the spare cases of coke and beer. The cans looked all right, but they were empty. I could hardly see the places where the paint was corroded. Now I understood why the bilge water was so brown.

March 31–April 3, 1991
Calms and sprinkling rain alternated, but I had a well calculated position: 20°40'S and 024°18'W. The daytime temperature reached 32° C (90° F). I started to live an owl's life... When the sun shone I hid in the cabin; in the dark I stayed out.

During the nights, I often watched the "TV." Lying on the deck I admired the infinite world of the stars. The sights sent me on a journey like a hypnotized medium. I seemed to see Lobo, the head of the wolf pack, who stretched his head toward the sky and started to howl. I saw myself too, but not in the present. As a member of a band with stone axes, I carried a block of salt packed in skins, and smelled the lightning-scorched savanna. Then the machine sped up, I rode a fast horse, maybe riding toward Augsburg.[48] In my leather pouch I carried dry meat ground between stones, which may not have been very different from *Salammbo*'s souppowders.

That juxtaposition brought me back to the present. I remembered the hypothesis of Captain Dr. Juba, who once said that the Hungarians wandering and venturing on land have common characteristics with the perennial voyagers of the seas. This theory was proven by the analysis of the Austro-Hungarian Navy's history. It showed, surprisingly, that not the Slavs, Dalmations, nor Italians, but the Hungarian sailors, coming from a landlocked country, were the best in the Navy, based on traditions of past ages. The wandering nomad and the oceangoing mariner had a common interest in the sky, which gives information and guidance for the traveler. It is possible that there is a certain ability of creative improvisation in our genes, which were once part of the tribes on the move.

---

[48] "I rode a fast horse, maybe riding toward Augsburg": A historical reference to the medieval Hungarian tribes in their raids of Western Europe. The Hungarians won an important victory near Augsburg in the early 10th century.

The mix of reality with the pictures of fantasy made these nights unique. A silence that I had not experienced before weighed on the ocean, air, and water. Peace permeated mind and matter. As the boat moved north, more familiar stars became visible. Taurus and Canis Major were getting higher, the Southern Cross and Centaur lower. Should I be happy or sad? In the starlight, homesickness was the winner... I longed for family, friends, and home. At the same time, my instincts seemed to dictate, "Don't push, it is a pity to leave Paradise too soon."

April 3-6, 1991
A windless period with light breezes. I had found such before only on the Mediterranean. On the 3rd, the boat stayed in one place, though I should have been in the Southeast Trades. I vented my anger against civilization, from atomic reactors to computerized robots to Saddam Hussein. If such well-established wind patterns were not reliable, there must be big trouble. I should clean my own backyard.

The reason for my pangs of conscience was the two tires I had thrown away. Used for drogues in the Roaring Forties, they were let go during the last day's cleaning and reorganizing. I had lightened *Salammbo*'s load, but not mine. I felt guilty for insulting the sea, so to ease my conscience I started all kinds of jobs. The light of the steering compass did not work. When I took it apart I saw that it had become a miniature salt pan. The fine salt had nearly squeezed the compass from its mount, eating up all the electrical connections. The repair took a whole day. Any inaccuracy could cause a fatal error. The compass was adjusted to the lubber line. I continued the inspection.

As for the lights, I used paraffin lamps for navigation. I was able to smile about the 25-liter (6.6-gallon) paraffin I had stored. Poor *Salammbo*, her deep draft was thanks to my caution in building her exceptionally strong and in carrying extra supplies. It is a fact that on a boat everything has a spare, even spares. Current was stored in a 145 AH main battery and 75 AH car starter battery; another 55 AH battery was used as a spare. Charging was provided by a wind generator, a solar panel, and the running of the boat's diesel. As backup I had oil and LP gas lamps, flashlights with alkaline batteries, a dynamo lamp, lightsticks, and candles. Looking back on the voyage, I realized that I had to use practically every tool and material I carried.

For example, the opening handle of the front Lewmar hatch failed. In the windless period, such failures were just enough to occupy my time. The small jobs filled the otherwise not too happy time.

On April 5 the usual speed returned—125 n. miles in 24 hours. The next day the wind stopped again, and I started the cursing. Everything is relative. I would have paid a fortune for this warmth on the 60° South parallel, in -5° C (23° F) and falling snow, amidst icebergs, driven by 60-knot winds. On the 7th of April the wind turned for the first time to the east, and then the southeast. Hopefully it was a true Trade Wind. My position: 10°46'S and 025°46' W.

We followed the progress of *Alba Regia* on our circle of radio operators. Nandi's position was 14°53'S and 037°30'W. Zsolt unwittingly made me angry. He proposed the game: "Who gets to the Equator first?" If I hadn't been sitting for 8 days in a windless bowl during Easter, I could have had a chance against the BOC. Right then I had a 300-mile advantage on Nandi, but this distance was equivalent to just a day's travel for the racers.

I lacked not only speed, but also gastronomic variety. I would have given my country for an apple, even for a lowly Jonathan. Since ketchup came closer to apple than mustard, I used it to flavor my plate of rice. It was a good thing that I liked rice. With the depletion of my supplies, it constituted the main part of my diet. To my great sorrow no flying fish landed on the deck of *Salammbo*.

I was still surprised at the absence of any life on the ocean. Maybe the quietness was the reason. I found out once again that regular radio connections have disadvantages. I learned not just the good, but also the bad news very promptly. I couldn't help anything or anybody; I could only gnaw at myself. According to the news, close acquaintances of mine had been involved in a car accident, and five of them had died. It cracked my spirit... they were those who had been anxious about me and my safety.

April 7-12, 1991

Salammbo progressed well again. I wondered for how long? The sky was clear, and 15- to 25-knot trade winds pushed the boat. It continued to be hot. My tactics were to drink only in the evening to prevent the sweating out of the liquid. On the 7th a good-natured bantering went on among the Equator club in Fehervar, *Alba Regia*, and *Salammbo*. Nandi complained about joint pains. I recommended my magic cure, the Richtofit sport cream. The air quickly filled up with commercials. Nandi corrected me at once; apparently the only effective medicine was the St. Jupat Helia Lotion. Then Karcsi grabbed the microphone—he suspected that *Salammbo* had perfected a universal elixir. I told him not yet, but that I did have a failsafe recipe for the overweight ones: a plate of rice daily, mixed with ketchup. Take it for two months on an open ocean trip.

A magnificent southeast wind would have carried me flying, but the wind vane oscillated on *Salammbo* as if it would like to dance a waltz with somebody. I was getting apoplectic; I couldn't tolerate detours. I steered by hand, mostly at night, because the sun scorched devastatingly. Sewing my recently torn Genoa occupied me during the day. It looked like my sails were disintegrating.

On the tenth of April a raven-like bird alighted on the dodger. With rusty memory I tried to recall Edgar Allen Poe's masterpiece. I was more successful in conjuring ghosts while looking at the tirelessly whirling dolphins, covered by capes woven from billions of phosphorescent plankton.

On April 14 my position was 01°56'S and 025°47'W. I still hadn't seen Polaris. The day's big event was a freighter crossing my path about 10 miles from *Salammbo*. It was the first steamer I had met since encountering the South Korean fishermen four months before.

There was great activity in the water and in the air. After sunset, two-foot-long fish flew out of the water like arrows. The flying fish followed low long paths, and the birds flew after them in a seemingly uncoordinated, impulsive way.

The following day a strong squall reached us. Dense rain with 25- to 30-knot gusts. The shower passed quickly, leaving a grand rainbow in the eastern sky. Then the clouds returned. I washed myself and my clothes in the lashing rain. Thanks to my new system of trapping rainwater, I collected 40 liters of drinking water in 10 minutes. My invention was really simple. I mounted a 10-foot rubber hose in the cheap canvas bucket I had purchased in Australia. The bucket hung on the end of the boom. After the rain had washed the salt off the sails, I put the end of the hose into a 5-gallon can.

According to my calculations, I crossed the Equator at 025°45'W, at about 1910 hours. Though Gibraltar was still far away, and Pola even farther, the circle around the globe was now closed. This was the tenth time I had crossed the Equator. Piroska congratulated me through the "Equator" station. In the festive hour the Fates sent another rain. At least I would not die of thirst...

April 13-16, 1991

It rained almost continuously for days. The bigger problem was that I was always hungry, and though I stuffed myself with rice and pasta, it did not diminish the hunger.

On the 13th I saw a bird on the deck. Its capture was not without danger, but I managed it. I was afraid that it might catch cold. In the afternoon the rain stopped, and I dried my guest in the cabin. It accepted the care, but not the food I offered. I let it go before sunset. Its takeoff was successful and it flew alright.

I was sure that I was in the northern hemisphere—the water drained the usual way, clockwise. *Salammbo* looked like it was anchored, with a complete calm and oily smooth seas. All the electric consumers were on hold. I tried the mechanical Walker log, but it sank vertically into the water.

I got out my moldy, soiled clothes. It was 55° C (131° F) on the deck, so I immediately fled back to the cabin's 40° C (104° F) relative cool. The sunny side of the boat was so hot it could burn. It was impossible to even freshen up in the water; it was 35° C (95° F). I went into the water anyway to check the bottom of the boat. It was smooth and entirely clean. Since I found no hitchhikers on it, I knew that the correct bottom paint had thankfully been found. It certainly contributed greatly to the high daily runs. Swimming around *Salammbo*, I was satisfied with the inspection. The boat looked a bit bow-heavy, so after getting back on deck I started re-ballasting by rearranging my supplies.

Above: *Ocean fashion in the searing heat of the Tropics—a sharp contrast from my attire in the Southern Latitudes just a few weeks earlier!*

Crossing the Doldrums went as predicted. The calm was interrupted by endless showers and lightning. During electrical storms, it was reassuring to think about the proper grounding of *Salammbo*'s mast and rigging.

Because of the energy shortage, the radio was my only consumer. I had shut everything else down. The wind generator went on strike, or only worked part-time. I had less than 40 liters (10.6 gallons) of diesel remaining, and there were still 2,314 n. miles to Gibraltar by the shortest route. I ruminated on the thought that although electrical gadgets make life easier for us, they are most bothersome when they have given up the ghost. It was no accident that I had substituted everything possible with more reliable mechanical devices. These were sometimes ridiculously simple. Instead of using a rudder angle indicator, I tied lines on the wheel rim to show the angle. The line tied to show the center position could be felt in any weather.

On April 16 my position was 04°16'N and 026°10'W. It was the end of taking it easy. The wind increased, but its direction was not convenient. I could hold only a 310° heading. In the evening I shared a radio connection with *Alba Regia*. Nandi was also in the Northern Hemisphere. His position was 005°46'W. He had an unpleasant incident. His front stay broke, and since he had no spare, he couldn't use his biggest jibs. He was understandably depressed. Zsolt and I tried to cheer him up.

I had now been underway for 10 months...

11

MUTINY ON BOARD SALAMMBO
(1991 April 17 — May 14)

"He who does not dare to risk does not accomplish anything at the right moment. Man, however, never takes risks if he is not confident that luck is with him."

—Napoleon

IN THE FOLLOWING DAYS, THE NORTHEAST TRADE WIND increased. The sea became choppy, and the wind heeled *Salammbo* to port. Since it seemed to be steady, I started to rearrange my stores once again, this time to starboard. It was difficult to shoot the sun—first because of the seas, and second because its altitude had increased. I figured that I would soon be under it. During the day temperatures reached 29-30° C (84-86° F), but the evening pail-bail still felt cool in the wind. I couldn't sleep in the cockpit anymore; my peaceful rests in that place were stopped by the weather and an unusual event.

EXCERPTS FROM THE LOG

April 18, 1991

At 1600 hours local time a ship of unidentifiable function arrived in my area. The poor visibility made it difficult to recognize, even with binoculars. The air was hazy and full of sand. In addition, the ship approached from the west, the direction of the setting sun. She sailed with the same speed as myself and kept the same course. When I got on the radio, she disappeared. I preferred to be alone.

April 19, 1991

Yesterday's ship appeared again and followed me like a bodyguard. I had no idea why she ambled there, when she could have easily gone at three times the speed of *Salammbo*. I guessed she was about 1000 tons, maybe a fishing boat or a research vessel. I still couldn't identify her. I wasn't wrong about the sand—the sails and antennas were full of it—even though we were at least 1000 miles from the Sahara. I didn't like the area; I would rather be farther away from West Africa's shores.

April 20, 1991

Position: 11°13'N and 028°49'W. Heading: 340°. Wind: East-Northeast, 30 knots.

The sea was rough. *Salammbo* sailed with the main and the storm jib.

The unknown ship approached between 1000 and 1100 hours, this time from the east, from the direction of the sun. I still could not establish her name or flag through the binoculars, but I noticed a few details in spite of the waves. She had a foremast and mid-bridge, and the rear deck was completely built up. I had seen all kinds of ships during my service as a mariner, but I still didn't know what to make of this one. I dismissed the idea of a research vessel. It occurred to me that the area around West Africa was known to be a dangerous place... a reputation earned not because of the weather, but due to the area's frequent and brutal pirate attacks.

I tried to contact her on the radio. I called on Channel 16 (VHF). No answer. I was getting angry. I had survived 80-knot storms and several-story-high waves, I had rounded the five Southern Capes, and I had escaped in one piece from the Roaring Forties and Furious Fifties. I hadn't hit icebergs or whales. I had suffered through 10 months. And then, just 2,000 miles from the finish, a dozen machine gun toting ruffians had spat in my soup. I could not leave it like that... So I prepared for the siege.

Looking out through a porthole, I worked fast. I put the shortwave radio on the 2182 MHz emergency calling frequency, and left the VHF on Channel 16. Then I loaded the flare gun. All ammunition was at hand. I readied the fire extinguishers and connected the spare bilge pump. Next I put combustible liquids, thinners, alcohol, and gasoline into glass bottles. After that, I poured the valuable contents of my last five wine bottles into plastic containers to create makeshift Molotov cocktails. Then I glued hand flares onto the side of the bottles. I prepared everything from firing positions to the first aid kit. In short order, *Salammbo* was battle-ready.

I recalled a similar preparation on the ship *Petőfi* when we were sailing into the Malacca Strait. Heeding advice given to us, we doubled the guards, mounted steel doors, and locked all the doors for the night. I remembered it mainly because the nightly lockup made my evening swimming training in the pool impossible. I also remembered how I had made some preparations myself… The first was to fix the sign reading "Purser" onto the door of the ship's most hated crew member.

If I was to expect an attack now, it would not be for the cashbox of my boat. The only valuable that might be coveted was the yacht herself, which with all of her equipment was worth around $100,000. She could be sold for about half her value on the black market. Therefore they had to get the boat intact, or else there would be no point in the attack. But in strong waves they could only approach with lifeboats. And against lifeboats I had a chance. In calm seas, they could stand by, and my only chance would be to start a fire on their ship.

The waves abated, but my companions didn't get any closer. Suddenly they made a 180° turn and started to leave. I couldn't understand it. Was it possible that I couldn't remain free from mirages? I was proud that I had lived these 10 months without visions or hallucinations. But now, just before the end, was I imagining colorful stories and seeing monsters? Going on deck, I saw a 25- to 30-thousand-ton ship on starboard. Had that been the reason for the swift departure of my mysterious stalkers? It was interesting that when the suspicious ship retreated, the approaching big ship also changed course and sailed away. I could not get them through the VHF, because my range was too small.

I was convinced that those on the freighter had surveyed the situation with professional sea-sense, and changed course to help *Salammbo*. Though I was relieved temporarily, I couldn't forget that if a motley crew had already followed me for three days, why wouldn't they soon resume it? I thought it would be a good idea to tell the home station. I asked Zsolt, on the Equator station, to inform MAHART and warn Zsuzsa to keep up my life insurance installments. I said this with some reluctance, as I was afraid of making a news sensation out of it. But the experts at MAHART didn't take my message lightly; they knew that piracy was a flourishing small-risk business. And they knew the reputation of the region. I heard on the radio that they sent telexes to the shipping agencies in the neighboring countries, giving *Salammbo*'s description and asking the agencies to notify their ships in the area.

Hearing the message made me feel better, but I was especially relieved when the wind rose to 40 knots from the northeast, whipping up the seas. I had never before been so happy to see bad weather. I hoped that I was losing not only the sun, but my followers as well.

April 21-26, 1991

Paradoxically, the weather continued to be favorable for me—that is to say, gales. I even enjoyed the unpleasant motion. Over-canvassing *Salammbo*, I drove the boat hard. I was hard on the east-northeast 38- to 40-knot wind, and despite the bearing and the waves breaking on the bow, we ran 128.5 miles on the 22nd. I was ahead of the sun, but I hoped that it was going to hurry north too, to broaden the Trade Wind zone. This would extend the favorable sailing conditions.

It seemed that the wind and waves had persuaded my stalkers to give up. In the following days both the wind and waves abated, but by that time I had gained enough of a lead. I thanked the hams of the Equator for their round-the-clock watch, and we returned to the regular daily periods. I also learned that the first two boats of the BOC had reached Newport, after finishing the Atlantic Ocean section in three weeks.

On the 26th I crossed the Tropic of Cancer in strong waves. It was still 1,500 miles to Gibraltar.

April 27-30, 1991

The weather made for a bad ending to the month. The wind came from the same direction, but increased to 40 knots. Two strands parted on the starboard lower shroud. After an exciting mast climb, I secured the damaged shroud with a 10mm Kevlar line. On the 28th I caught a full moon gale. The sleeping bag came out again, because the temperature was dropping fast. The next day the wind fluctuated, trying my nerves. I had to reef the sails eight times in four hours.

I had started exactly four months ago from Australia, so my impatience could be excused. It was the end of the Trades, and the Variables came next.[49] I had reason to be concerned about the Azores High. Therefore I sailed close to the wind as much as I could in order to skirt it on the east. Calms and storm fronts came one after the other, infuriating me. I got my anger in check, avoided throwing the sextant into the water, and instead jumped in myself. Cooled by the bath, I climbed back aboard. And then, miracle of miracles, the wind steadied.

On April 30 the month ended on the calendar, but according to the weather I was still in the middle of it. All kinds of winds blew from 0 to 40 knots, with the direction changing every quarter of an hour. The calms, squalls, rain, and confused seas tried me to no end. Not only was the wind crazy, but I was also afraid that I had gone mad myself. Finally, I sighted a freighter. She could have been 5-8 miles away, but I couldn't reach her on the VHF. I could hardly stop myself from kicking something. It was a good thing that I still had some self-control; I could have done more damage to

---

[49] "It was the end of the Trades, and the Variables came next": Referring to particular global wind patterns, which vary as one travels north or south.

Salammbo than the Roaring Forties had. There were 1,200 miles to Gibraltar, but it seemed like more than the 30,000 I had covered so far.

May 1-3, 1991

Mutiny on the *Salammbo*... The maddeningly whimsical weather induced a riot on board. The mutiny was successfully suppressed, but not without casualty. My favorite cap slammed into the water and sank slowly to the bottom. I had never been so far from land or people for so long, and extreme loneliness came over me. The lousy, meager food and the constant sail handling caused a tension that even stopped me from reading. When I planned the trip, I had taken into account the possibility of capsize or piracy, but not mutiny. No doubt the greatest danger for me now was my own self.

On May 2 I ran out of my chocolate stock, which was the last coloring and improving agent to make the plain rice and pasta more consumable. The good news was that Nandi had reached Newport. Dark clouds came at night, and the wind reached 50-60 knots. The Pilot Charts didn't indicate gales in this sector. Naturally the swells increased to maximum, and remained stormy for days.

The radio waves were quieter. They announced other big storms in quiet, measured summaries. The broadcast from "My Homeland" was about Cardinal Mindszenty, with László Mensaros' comments.[50] Mensaros labeled the Communists' actions as Satan's own, which reminded me of President Reagan, who had called the Communist Soviet Union the evil empire. I had never considered before that Reagan reminded me of Churchill. I believe that we Hungarians, with the rest of Eastern Europe, should be very thankful for the eight years of his presidency. The broadcast following Mindszenty's funeral was finished with the thoughts of László Mecs, which took me back to my childhood. I saw in front of me the round-faced, white-haired Uncle Laci, as he discussed the possibility of me furthering my studies in Pannonhalma. It was a pity that the decision was not up to him and me.[51] I could not spend much time with the sweet memories of that discussion in the shade of the walnut tree. I was headed

---

[50] József Cardinal Mindszenty was the leader of the Catholic Church in Hungary from 1945 through 1973. He escaped to the U.S. Embassy in Budapest during the Russian invasion in 1956. László Mensaros was a famous and prolific Hungarian actor whose career spanned from the 1950s until his death in 1993.

[51] "...the possibility of me furthering my studies in Pannonhalma": I yearned for the chance to go to this excellent school, but it was not a feasible option for political reasons. My father was working for a state-owned shipping company, and I could not risk hurting his standing among the Communist leaders who controlled his career. We knew that his reputation could easily be jeopardized if I were to attend a Church-owned school.

for exciting hours. In the dismal weather I approached the island of Santa Maria of the Azores Archipelago.

May 5, 1991

I spent the whole night at the wheel, but fortunately the wind abated towards dawn, 0800 hours local time. I could just see the eastern point of Santa Maria. Not much later I passed beside a rock, 30 feet high and partly awash. It was the first land I had seen since Cape Horn, and I had arrived there with an accuracy within one mile, despite bad visibility. I was flushed with pride. But the mood was dampened when half of my lower left wisdom tooth broke off. This was probably due to my incessant chewing of gum, which had replaced—for lack of proper food—breakfast, lunch, and dinner.

At the eastern corner of Isla Sao Miguel I turned right, directly towards Gibraltar. The wind settled down to 25-30 knots, and I went to sleep after setting all my alarm clocks to half hour rest periods. I had only slept 40 minutes in the last 24 hours, but I was afraid that I might run aground if the wind shifted. I don't know whether I was awakened by the alarm clocks or by the unusual motion of the boat, but I jumped out of my sleeping bag and tore open the hatch. I was heading west—that is, towards the islands. It occurred to me that Chichester's famous circumnavigating boat, the Gipsy Moth IV, ended up that way (with somebody else sailing it). It was very fortunate that I woke up in time. What was difficult to understand was how the wind had not turned. The wind vane had somehow allowed *Salammbo* to turn around; it was very disquieting that it would inexplicably fail me now, when it could have easily led to disaster. I used some vehement, but improper expressions on Mother's Day.

WE FULFILLED OUR DUTY

The weather belied every prediction for the second week in May. The Pilot Chart showed only one or two gales for that period, and though it was the first one that hit us, it lasted an entire week. The wind didn't drop below 40 knots; one time it even hit 55. I had to sail the boat close to the wind in the short, steep seas in order to go in the right direction. For *Salammbo*, it was like the final lash of the crop on the horse's flank before the finish line. Here we should have had westerly winds for a while, but instead we fought northeast gales for days. Clouds prevented me from making celestial measurements, and I was drenched at every attempt. The temperature dropped to 13° C (55° F). The water came through the hatch again and washed over my bed.

On May 8, I was 618 miles from Gibraltar. By that point I felt like I could have walked that far on one leg. On one leg maybe, but not without a mast. The continual pressure took its toll: the 16mm (5/8") shackle that had been holding one of the headstays and the tack of the jib sheared off. I couldn't believe my eyes. Fortunately the other stay still held. I had time to fix the mast with spare halyards, so I waited for the waves to abate. Ultimately I had to turn away from the wind to change the damaged part, while cobwebbing the mast with spare lines. The action required considerable effort, but was ultimately a great success. I was filled with a childish happiness that even such a specially manufactured part had a spare.

By May 10, my pantry only had some rice left, and my increasing hunger was not helped by the knowledge that I was still 396 miles from the Strait. The ocean started to become populated again, and I met ships more often. One morning I was entertained to an air show. I presumed that it was the British Air Force from Gibraltar. The proximity of Europe was also demonstrated in less pleasant ways... *Salammbo* sailed amongst garbage thrown around by the waves.

I received happy news over the radio. MAHART and Ganz-Danubius had arranged a new sizable financial contribution to cover my expected expenses in Gibraltar. My friend Walter Speer had also sent a spinnaker to hasten my trip home. Learning of the help of my supporters aided me in covering the last miles, as I made preparations for the long-awaited mooring. When the weather permitted, I cleaned and washed in rainwater. I prepared the flags and studied the charts and currents in the Strait.

I did not want to reef and slow the boat down. I preferred to stay half days at the helm and maintain the speed. It was a crowning success. I maintained a 7- to 8-knot average, but I was close to collapse from exhaustion. At that point I needed not only to keep my strength up, but also to have good luck until I reached the shores.

On May 12 at 0230 hours a freighter of 8,000-10,000 tons wanted to cross in front of me, then behind me, and again in front. Her first maneuvers were suspect, so I started the motor in time. Even so, I was only able to avoid her by backing the jib. The next day, at 0330 hours, a container ship nearly wiped me out. On her approach I fired up *Salammbo*, but even with the revved up motor I only avoided the collision by a few meters. It underscored that the greatest danger to *Salammbo* on the circumnavigation came from men rather than nature. Under the circumstances there was no question that I had the right of way, yet the captains of the ships did nothing to prevent a collision. I have never had any racist tendencies, but this time, on Channel 16, I did several times very emphatically refer to the person's supposedly tropical origin.[52]

The traffic started to resemble that of a narrow shipping lane. There was

---

[52] "I did several times very emphatically refer to the person's supposedly tropical origin": This form of insult alludes to a jab at some shipping companies that attempt to maximize their profits by hiring cheap (and notoriously less skilled) deckhands from a variety of tropical locations.

no question about needing sleep, but in 72 hours I had slept only for 3. According to my calculations, Gibraltar Harbor was only 55.2 miles ahead of me. I was excited that I could reach it that night. After I underwent a quick wash and shave, the wind—exceptionally—started to blow from the right direction. Still in daylight, the magnificent moment arrived. Halfway between Cadiz and Trafalgar I sighted land: the continent of Europe. The proximity of the finish line did not only fulfill the greatest challenge of my life, but it also meant the ending of a dream and an era.

The blissful feeling of victory grabbed me, and as I was nearing Cape Trafalgar, my thoughts turned to the famous sea battle. "We won," Nelson had praised his comrades, "because every Englishman did his duty."

Is that all there was to say about the exceptionally heroic battle, or was it the typical English understatement? No! Nelson could not have said anything more appropriate at the time. To fulfill one's duty is the most anyone can do. Important contributions to the British victory included the heroes' determination, their fighting valor, and often their exemplary sacrifices.

Yet there were other necessary ingredients as well. Victories are achieved at a certain time and place, but they start much earlier and in other places. In this historical example, the victory at Trafalgar started years, even decades earlier, with the ship's design, the growth of the shipbuilding industry—and because of its complexity, the whole of English industry— the integrity of the Admiralty, and the training of the officers and seamen to the highest standards.

Heroic efforts are often of the moment. They may bring success, but could just as well result in martyrdom. The history of Hungary is an example of that. Few succeeded in organizing the people to discharge their duties with lasting success. The greatest Hungarians went mad attempting it. This endeavor is very difficult, even for more geographically cohesive nations.

Relating this to *Salammbo*, it is possible that with greater sacrifice, and less conscientious and time-consuming preparations, the victory could still have been achieved. But then again, the most important thing was that *Salammbo* maintained her functional integrity. This was despite the unfavorable circumstances and the many mishaps, and without requiring external help to complete the voyage as her skipper planned. The journey was completed with difficulties, but without heroism.

Although I found my discursive thoughts upon glimpsing Cape Trafalgar to be a little too exalted, the thing that came to my mind at that time was Churchill's sentence announcing another victory: "We shall thank God for the noblest of his blessings, for the knowledge that we did our duty."

The Lord took my musings to be premature. The dream of that day's arrival was shattered by calm.

EXCERPTS FROM THE LOG
May 14, 1991

I drifted slowly towards the strait. It was past midnight when I reached Tarifa. With the apathy of an exhausted man, I recognized that the wind had picked up and then graduated to a 45-knot gale right on the nose. It lasted until morning. But the painful tacking seemed to last forever on the aggressively short and hard waves. I had to gather all my strength, and all my tricks, so that I could stay awake, and up at the wheel, and avoid the commercial shipping. Because of the inclement weather, several ships gave way to *Salammbo*, as if they guessed that not only every mile, but every yard was important to her.

I had been on my feet for the fourth day straight, four and a half months out of Australia. Therefore it was unbelievable that The Rock was suddenly in front of me, and I was sailing to the corner of the Bay of Gibraltar. I had a scant 2 liters of diesel left, but I proceeded slowly and carefully to the Immigration and Customs Dock. As I stepped onto the pier I hung onto *Salammbo*'s lifeline, and I could not let go. An agent arrived, tied up *Salammbo*, and invited me into the office. I walked uncertainly. I was happy when I could sit down. The official asked the usual questions, and when he heard that my last port of call had been Fremantle, he sat down himself. He didn't ask any more questions, but filled out the entry forms, escorted me back to the boat, and helped me to untie the lines.

I motored back to my same slip from one year before with my last cupful of fuel, and tied up like one merely returning from an early morning fishing trip. It was 7:00 in the morning, and everything was closed and empty. I collected enough change to call Zsuzsa. The call was successful, but when the money ran out, I told the rest to the empty phone booth. Back on the boat I sat behind the wheel. I put my feet up on the seat and gazed from under the visor of my cap at the sun rising over the forest of masts. I didn't want to eat or drink, I didn't crave a hot shower, I didn't miss anything I had planned to do in the last hours, weeks, or months. I just sat in the boat with one hand on the wheel and thought of nothing. Nothing at all! It might have been the first time that it had ever happened to me. I had never thought that this numb, thoughtless state could be so fantastically pleasant.

Above: *I made it! Just after my arrival in Gibraltar—*
able to rest at last after fulfilling my dream.

I sat motionless in the boat for nearly two hours. Towards nine o'clock, the harbor started to wake up, and things started moving. I received word that there were phone messages for me in the marina office—my wife, daughter, and friends were calling. The "daytime" broadcast switched the conversation to the air. I tried to speak in a coherent way that they could comprehend, but I was near collapse from exhaustion. I exchanged my leftover Australian dollars and went to sit in a pizzeria. There I ordered pizza and salad, ate the pizza with chicken, and drank my beer. I ordered ice cream too, but left it uneaten. It was better to be on the boat, where I climbed, in slow motion, into my coffin-bunk. I was home. I had arrived.

EPILOGUE

$S_{ALAMMBO}$ STARTED FOR HOME FROM GIBRALTAR ON MAY 23, 1991. I wasn't alone on the boat for this part, which lasted over three weeks. I sailed in the company of my friend Andris Lovas, through both weak and high winds, towards the first and last harbor of my voyage: Pola. On June 16, just minutes after 10:00am, I moored at the same pier where I had started from a year before.

My family members were waiting for me, as were my friends. Many of them had stood by me throughout the whole undertaking. The meeting was complete with laughs and tears; it was a truly unforgettable celebration. With this, a long voyage and an unusual adventure came to an end.

St. Jupat, *Salammbo*, *Alba Regia*, the Equator Club... a dumping of Hungarian sailboats on the seas? I wouldn't be surprised if the reader were confused by the names.

After all was over, the question remained: "What is this circumnavigation thing about? What is it good for?" As the old saying goes, "Navigare necesse est, vivere non est necesse"?[53] Kossuth directed Hungarians towards the seas, but many still take the news of a new

---

[53] "Navigare necesse est, vivere non est necesse": Latin expression meaning "To sail is necessary; to live is not necessary"—a reference to the ancient Roman story of Pompey's daring and heroic leadership at sea, ordering his men to sail onward with the grain they were carrying home from Africa, in spite of their fear of the terribly stormy conditions they faced.

circumnavigation with incredulity.[54]

I must start the explanation from further back. It is obvious today that no inland country can exist without ties to the seas. The role of the oceans in transportation, food distribution, and communication is not new, but now an ever-increasing part of our raw materials come this way. The overpopulation of the continents turns the people's interest to the seas in order to enlarge their living area.

Above: *My friends welcome me back to Pola. My good friend Jozsef Gal (one of the two crew members to circumnavigate on the St. Jupat) presents me with the victory cup in honor of my achievement.*

What does this have to do with ocean sailing, individual performance, and world travel? I can answer this from my own point of view, without claiming to represent the beliefs of Jozsef Gal or Nandi Fa. We are not only observers of the world's events, but participants in them as well. In the time of nationalism and separatism, it is paradoxical but true that today's man has to be a citizen of the world. Divisions between countries become blurred in many respects, such as international concern about whaling, ecology, and conservation. The oceans are a shared resource. Everybody has equal rights to the open seas. It is of common interest to use and preserve them. In the area of interest and protection, the Hungarians'

---

[54] Kossuth: A reference to Lajos Kossuth (1802-1894), often called "the Father of Hungarian Democracy," who urged Hungarians toward seagoing enterprises because of their commercial importance.

Above: *Lifted up by my friends after my arrival in Pola.*

distance from the sea shrinks our possibilities, but not our rights.

I feel that it is important to make my compatriots conscious of these facts, to promote the spirit of creative expansion of their endeavors. We shall courageously step over the boundaries of our narrowed borders to know the world and prove our abilities. We live in the time of enterprises. Its inexhaustible medium is the sea, and the exploration of the sea is still just as interesting as space research. But it is important that whatever we start, we shall do it as Hungarians, returning home to finish it.

Sailing is not only my hobby; it is my trade. *Salammbo*'s voyage around the globe can therefore be viewed as pursuing my craft. In addition, without setting out to do so, I achieved the world record for the speed of my circumnavigation for a boat of *Salammbo*'s size.[55] *Salammbo* is not a racer; her designer intended her as a lake and/or coastal cruiser. Yet because of the 11-year sunspot cycle maximum and the cyclone activity it induced at the time of my voyage, the boat covered the thirty-six thousand nautical miles extraordinarily fast.

Salammbo's voyage was a true challenge of man and his knowledge. I had the strongest desire to know what I was capable of, what I was worth. The planned course offered the necessary grade of difficulty. My personal motivations may have seemed selfish and egotistic, and perhaps they partially were. But *Salammbo* sailed under the Hungarian flag, starting and

---

[55] My daily average of 125 n. miles in the course of completing a circumnavigation via the five southernmost capes was the fastest for a boat *Salammbo*'s size (only 31' long).

finishing in Hungary, taking an honorable place with her performance in the annals of sailing history. In this respect it was a message for my compatriots and the rest of the world as well: proving that with proper preparation and tenacity, there is no impossible task, even in spite of unfavorable circumstances. Believing this restores our self-esteem and prompts us to action.

Above: *My friends threw me in the water, but I managed to keep a firm grip on my celebratory champagne!*

The word "enterprise" has to be discussed too. It conjures thoughts of business. I knew even in the preparatory stages that my voyage would be an amateur enterprise, despite the professional execution on the shipping side. I was among those who left without sponsors, and couldn't enjoy the sizable benefits of advertising campaigns or business concerns. My enterprise could benefit the sailing programs under my direction on Lake Balaton, but only in an indirect way. Yet the yearlong voyage, and the frequent depression and other hardships it entailed, still made me richer— in my feelings, self-confidence, and reflective experiences. With its own brand of shock therapy, it corrected my system of values. And most importantly, it presented me with the opportunity to become acquainted with a world that is savagely hard, but free of any malevolence.

Coming home, I found that the measures changed again. Man is not free from the influences of the environment. Its character and individuality can shrink or expand. A dream was fulfilled, and though I imagined the awakening differently, the magician did not break his wand. Now I am driven by new dreams, by the hope that personal and social matters can be organized in my home country in the wake of the destruction of the Berlin Wall. Whether it will be successful I don't know. Regardless, I will do my duty.

Despite the fact that I live in the countryside, near Lake Balaton, my contact with nature has shrunk. In the mornings I run the usual circles on the slopes of Oreghegy. The Vödör valley opening up in the rays of the rising sun gives me the only chance to remind myself of the albatrosses gliding into the thoughts of the waves. This is the way I trained before my voyage, timing it for the evenings, so that my eyes could get used to the dark. But right now I need light. If I don't see the sun getting into the Vödör valley, *Salammbo* may well prepare for another voyage.

Above: *The closest family circle—embracing my wife and daughter for the first time in six months.*

THANK YOU

Thank you for sharing in my journey by reading this book! If you enjoyed it, I would greatly appreciate it if you would leave a review on my amazon.com sales page.

There are many exciting events on the horizon. I am working on translating my second book, *Kihivas II: From the Szilas Creek to the Connecticut River*. It chronicles my adventures since completing my first circumnavigation in 1991, including various races, a second circumnavigation, and my big move from Hungary to the United States.

I am also now in the hunt for sponsors as I prepare for my third circumnavigation, as an entrant in the Golden Globe Race 2018. The GGR will be a nonstop race around the world in which competitors are only allowed to use technology comparable to that used on the first nonstop circumnavigation in 1968. It is certain to be my greatest challenge yet!

For updates on all of this and more, please visit my website at **www.koparsailing.com**.

ACKNOWLEDGEMENTS

My enterprise was only virtually solo. Many contributed to its success. They were the reason to write my story, repaying some of my debt. Without them and their help, *Salammbo* couldn't have finished her voyage, or maybe she couldn't have even started out. Like all lists, this one may not be complete. I have to ask the forgiveness of those who are unintentionally omitted.

MY HELPERS WERE:

The Anderle family, Anthony Calleja, Bajusz Károly, Balogh Dezső, Bárd László, Bátki Sándor, Bátaszéki Judit, Bársony György and Tamás, Benke Zsuzsanna, Béni Gyöngyi, Dr. Berger Iván, Dr. Biczi Éva, Boros Béla, Bruckner János, Bruckner József, Dr. Büchler János, Chris Mews, Christa Burger, Charlie, Cittel Lajos, Csaba László and his wife, Cservenka Ernő, Csoma János, Csúr Endre, Csellei László, Dán László, Dárdai Zoltán, Debreceni József, Deli Sándor, Dirnitrisz, Drobni Nándor, Egyed Gyula, Erdős Gábor, Eszéki Tamás, Fa Nándor, Dr. Farkas Anikó, Fekecs Imre, Filipovics László, Dr. Földi József, Fogarasi László, Gál József, Georg Burger, Géczy István, Göbl Anikó, Dr. Guszter Géza, Győri Miklós, Hajdú Benjamin, Herke Géza, Hercegh Béla, Hódosi Ilona, Horthy András, Horváth Imre, Horváth László, Horváth Oszkár, Horváth Péter, Dr. Horváth János and his wife, Dr. Hudomel Norbert and his wife, Huszár Viktor, Inge Uibel, Jandrasek Sándor, John Royce, John Showel, Dr. Juba Ferenc, Kamarás István, Kazínczy László, Dr. Kádár György and Kristóf, Dr. Kerpán István, Kerpán Anikó, Kiss László, Kiss Pál, Király László— Senior and Junior, Kovács János, Kovács Erzsébet, Kovács Róbert, Konkoly Zoltán, Kovács Attila, Dr. Kratochwill Balázs, Lovas András, Légárd László, Louice Schultz, Dr. Malárics Viktor, Michel Jan, Miltényi

Dénes, Mészáros Tibor and his wife, and András, Mrázik Marianna, Nagyváradi János, Nyemcsek Károly, Patakfalvi Gábor, Pál István, Pál Jenő, Pál Zsolt, Peter Fletcher, Praveen M. Thanki, Pusztay József, Rádics János, Rády László, Raffai György, Reindl László, the Reisch family, Dr. Rohonyi András, Rühl Lajos, Sárkány Erika, Sárközi Péter, Serfözo' László, Somody Pálné and Péter, Soós Miklós, Sörös Jenő, Stefan Aschenbrenner, Speer Walter, Suhajda Olivér, Sulyok Miklós, Szentváry Lukács György, Szilágyi István, Szitnyai Jenő, Dr. Szilbereki József, Szabó Péter, Seppo Sausti, Szöllősy Ágnes, Sümeg Katalin, Szűcs Jűzsef, Taszler István, Terdi Attila, Tóth Ferenc, Török András, Tőzsér István, Ursula Gratza, the Vajda family, Vajtai Lajos, Ventur Jürgen, Viszt János, Visy László, Walter Klobas, Wattay Antal/Richárd, Werner Gram, Dr. Zajkás Gábor, Zácsik Tamás, Zsigmond Iván, Zsolt Róbert.

MY SPONSORS WERE:
Magyar Hitel Bank, Magyar Hajózási Részvénytársaság, Csepel Autó, Műszaki Anyag- és Gépkereskedelmi Vállalat, Ganz-Danubius Trading Company, Mátrapack Mátraaljai Állami Gazdaság, Prior Agrárinnovációs Kisszövetkezet, Equator Club, Atlas Insurance, Délker, Magyar Honvédség Élelmezési és Ruházati Szolgálati Fönöksége, Műanyagipari Kutatóintézet Szolgáltató Kft., Hoffmann La Roche Wien, Tucker Fastener Ltd. Birmingham, Uljanik Pula, Heavy Special.

Special thanks to the translators of the original Hungarian book, Istvan Geczy and Ian Shires, whose selfless, hard work was the foundation of this book.

ABOUT THE AUTHOR

Istvan Kopar was born in Budapest, Hungary, in 1953. He worked as a seaman for MAHART (Hungarian Shipping Company) from 1971 to 1984. He started his own marina/charter operation and sailing school in Europe in the 1980s. Since relocating to the United States in 1994, Kopar has worked as an operational manager of a vessel recovery company, a teacher at Sea School in Fort Lauderdale, Florida, an instructor trainer for U.S. Sailing, and the Sailing Master at Seawanhaka Corinthian Yacht Club in New York. After his solo circumnavigation, Kopar competed in a number of prestigious blue water races. He completed his second circumnavigation in 1997, as skipper of the winning boat in the Hong Kong Challenge Round the World Race. Kopar holds a B.S. in Maritime Studies from the Technical University of Budapest, as well as a B.S. in Economics/Foreign Trade from the College for Foreign Trade at Budapest. He has authored two books: *Kihivas: Alone at the Ends of the Earth*, and *Kihivas II: From the Szilas Creek to the Connecticut River*. Kopar became a naturalized U.S. citizen in 2000. He is fluent both in English and his native Hungarian. He has two adult daughters, and currently lives with his wife in Boca Raton, Florida.

ABOUT THE EDITOR

Robert Farrelly was born and raised on the north shore of Long Island, New York. He first met Istvan Kopar while earning his certification as a U.S. Sailing instructor, when Kopar was his instructor trainer. Farrelly has worked as a sailing instructor, lifeguard, camp waterfront director, college cross country coach, and high school track coach. He taught U.S. History & Government for several years at his alma mater, St. Anthony's High School, before leaving to explore the world of writing and editing. While editing the English translation of *Kihivas*, Farrelly worked closely with Kopar to ensure that Kopar's voice was properly preserved. He finds Istvan Kopar's story to be particularly inspiring, and hopes that it will resonate with many readers. Farrelly holds a B.A. in History and Secondary Education from the College of the Holy Cross in Worcester, Massachusetts. He is fluent in English, and knows approximately one or two words of Hungarian.

Made in the USA
Middletown, DE
16 November 2015